Hamilton Beach Electric Panini Press Grill Cookbook

200 Easy, Tasty, and Healthy Panini Press Recipes for Beginners and Advanced Users

Seana Currt

Table of Contents

Introduction

The Hamilton Panini Press Grill is one of the simple and versatile cooking appliances available in the market. It looks simple but attractive and having non-stick cooking surfaces on the top and bottom cooking surface area. It comes with a compact size and doesn't take much space over your kitchen top. It is capable to hold 2 to 3 sandwiches at a time over its 10 inches by 8-inch cooking surface area. It is one of the safest cooking appliances comes with a large cool-touch pressing handle on its top lid portion. The outer portion of the appliances comes with a nice chrome finish. It cooks your sandwiches faster and also saves your cooking time and efforts.

The Hamilton Panini grill comes with two light indicators one is red and another is green. When you power the plug into power socket the red light illuminates. When the grill reaches its desire preheating temperature the green light illuminates. Your Hamilton Panini press is capable to grill perfect sandwiches with perfection. It is an ideal cooking appliance for making long bread sandwiches and equipped with a floating lid which allows you to press the sandwiches of any size.

This cookbook contains tasty, healthy and delicious Panini recipes selected from the different categories like breakfast Panini's, vegetable Panini's, poultry Panini's, Beef & lamb Panini's, pork Panini's, bruschetta, burgers & pizza and miscellaneous. All these recipes are unique and written into an easily understandable form. All the recipes come with preparation and cooking time information. The book also contains step by step information with cooking instructions. Finally, all the recipes end with their nutritional value information. The nutritional value information will help you to keep track of daily calorie intake. There are various books available in the market on this topic thanks for choosing my book. I hope you love and enjoy all the tasty and healthy recipes written in this book.

Chapter 1: Basics of Hamilton Beach Electric Panini Press Grill

What is Hamilton Beach Electric Panini Press Grill?

The Hamilton Beach Electric Panini Press Grill is one of the economical Panini press grill available in the market. The Hamilton Beach Panini grills come with the large cooking surface area. It is capable of making 2 to 3 sandwiches at a single cooking cycle. It also helps to make tasty quesadillas, sweet fruit turnovers and more. The Hamilton Beach Panini press grill is an ideal choice for a large family. It has a floating lid which helps to evenly press the sandwiches from any size and thickness. It allows you to make your favourite sandwiches without hold down the lid while cooking cycle. It gives even cooking results without burning your food.

While using Hamilton Panini press you never need to flip your sandwiches. The upper and lower non-stick cooking grid area of the sandwich maker is heated equally which gives you warm, even, and crisp result. The Panini press comes with the light indicator when you preheat your Panini press 6 minutes before placing your food. The green light will illuminate to indicate that your Panini press is preheated and ready to cook your sandwich, quesadillas and more. The top lock hinge on Panini lid helps to cook your favourite pizza or bruschetta without touching the top side over the food surface. The hinge lock allows you to adjust the height of the top lid while cooking. It requires small space over your kitchen top due to its compact size and the upright storage will easily fit into your kitchen countertop or cabinet. It is one of the perfect kitchen gadgets for your small kitchen.

The Hamilton Panini press comes with 10 inch by 8-inch non-stick cooking grid surfaces which ensure that your food is cooked without sticking food over the grid. The non-stick cooking grids add other health benefits to those people who love crispy grilled food but also worried about extra calorie consumption. The Hamilton Panini grill cooks your food with fewer fats and oil without compromising the taste or flavour of the food.

How to Use Hamilton Beach Electric Panini Press Grill?

The Hamilton Panini Grill is easy to operate it doesn't come with ON / OFF buttons or any other temperature control. When you plug it into a power socket and on the power switch Hamilton Panini grill starts working. The step by step operating instruction is given below will help you to cook your food using Hamilton Panini press grill cooking appliances.

1. Plug your Hamilton Beach Electric Panini grill power cord into a power socket. The

red light will illuminate continue until you unplug your Panini gill from the power socket.

2. Before placing your food into Panini always preheats your Panini grill for 6 minutes or until the green light illuminates. The green light will illuminate automatically when the desire cooking temperature reached.
3. Then spay cooking surface area with the help of cooking spray. Then place your bread slices at the bottom surface of the grid. Then place the sandwich ingredients such as vegetables, pre-cooked meats, spices, cheese and spreads. Then top another bread slice and turn lower the lid.
4. Do not press the cover use cover locking knob to lock the cove at desire height.
5. Then wait for 3 to 5 minutes, use hand mitts to unlock the lid and lift the lid to check your food is cooked properly as per your requirements. If not then again lock the lid and wait for 1 to 2 minutes.
6. Open the lid and check your sandwich if it is ready to serve then places it into serving plate. Do not cut the sandwich over non-stick grid surface.
7. Unplug the Hamilton Panini grill from the power socket and let it cool down before cleaning it.

Which Bread to Choose for Panini?

To choose the right bead for Panini is depends upon what kind of sandwich you want to make into your Panini grill. To choose the perfect bread for your sandwich you also need to consider the ingredients you want to use in bread. If you are using the soft and moist stuffing's or fillings then denser and dryer bread is one of the best choices for your sandwich. The dry bread soaks the moisture present in the fillings.

- Bread for making dry Panini

If you want to add little weight ingredients, melting cheese or lean meat into your favourite sandwich then you have to choose dry Panini bread-like Brioche, flatbread, challah, rye, artisan bread(thin slice), pita and multigrain bread.

- Bread for making wet Panini

If you are using weight ingredients like tomato, packed moisture-filled meats, Italian beef and other wet ingredients then you need to choose strong solid sturdy bread. The best bread options for weight Panini are focaccia, baguette, hard rolls, sourdough(thick cuts), ciabatta and artisan bread(thick cut)

List of Popular Bread Types

There are several Panini bread options are available which are the perfect choice for making

Panini grill sandwiches. The list of some popular Panini beads is:

- Italian bread: Italian bread is having a shorter and wider loaf. It is similar to French bread, loaf created into the water instead of milk. Italian bread has crusty yeast loaf typically plumper and shorter than French bread.
- Baguette: A long crisp-crusted French bread typically having 26 inches long and 3 inches wide in size and it is made up from basic lean dough. Mostly these beads are used for making sandwiches.
- French bread: A French bread is crusty, light yeast bread basically made using water instead of milk. The bread is crusty from outside and having light and soft crumb. These beads are made into different shapes and sizes.
- Sourdough Bread: This is one of the best alternatives for conventional bread. Due to the bread is lower in phytate makes it nutritious and easily digestible.

What bread to avoid?

Avoid typically processed and sliced white bread while making a Panini grill sandwich. The white bread is light and airy not suitable for grilling these bread are used for making cold sandwiches. The bagel is made up of tough and chewy crust so it is not the right choice for making Panini.

Hamilton Panini Press Tips

1. Fillings come out

This is happening due to many reasons the first reason is stuffing too many ingredients into a sandwich. To avoid this you must stuff your sandwich with at least two cold cuts, vegetable slices and easy fillings.

If you are using Low-quality bread, fillings come out because the bread is less dense and thin. To avoid this use thick bread slices and coats it with peanut butter.

The cheese holds the ingredients if you are not using cheese then strong chances of fillings will come out.

2. Uneven cooking results

Sometimes you notice that the uneven cooking results. Your sandwich is not properly cooked, this is happening due to your Hamilton Panini press grill as not preheated properly. Before placing your sandwich into Panini press make sure the grill surface is heated properly to get even cooking results.

3. Soggy bread

This problem exists because of using an excess liquid such as water, oil or sauce into your sandwiches. If you use excess wet ingredients it will make your sandwich soggy and no one wants to eat soggy bread. To avoid this use little water, souse or oil while making your sandwich. If vegetables and meat hold extra moisture or water then drain it properly before placing it into your sandwich.

4. For getting the crunchy result

To make your sandwich crunchy from outside then brush olive oil or melted butter over the bread on the outside area. If you are using wet ingredients like tomato slice then place it into the centre with cheese or meat.

5. Cooking tougher cuts of meats

Before placing tougher meat for cooking always remember to tenderize the meat to keep it overnight marinade using vinegar or wine.

Benefits of Using Hamilton Beach Electric Panini Press Grill

The Hamilton Panini Press Grill comes with various types of benefits some of the important benefits are given as follows:

1. Make healthy meals

If you are vegetarian and following any diet then Hamilton Panini press is an ideal cooking tool for you. Using Panini press you can easily make veggie sandwiches. The Hamilton Panini press comes with the non-stick cooking surface so you require less oil or no oil to grill your sandwiches. Less oil means fewer calories consumed.

2. Simple to use

The Hamilton Panini press is one of the affordable appliance available in the market. It doesn't have any ON / OFF button or any temperature control knob. You just need to plug it and the Panini press is ready to make your sandwich. Place your sandwich in Panini press grill and wait for some minutes. Your healthy, tasty and delicious sandwich is ready for servings.

3. Not only grill but also help to prepare a variety of other dishes

The Hamilton Panini press not only makes tasty and delicious sandwiches. It is also capable to make an omelette, bruschetta, pizza, quesadillas, grilled any vegetables and more with the help of Hamilton Panini grill you can cook different dishes.

4. Easy to clean

The Hamilton grill comes with non-stick cooking grids due to non-stick layer it is easy to clean. You just need to clean it with the help of a damp cloth.

Cleaning and Maintenance

A simple step by step cleaning instruction is given below will help you to clean your Hamilton Panini Press Grill easily.

1. Before start cleaning process unplugs your Hamilton Panini Press grill from the power socket and lets it allow to cool down at room temperature.
2. Take a paper towel and wipe out both the cooking surface to clean and remove the drippings.
3. To remove the food residue use wooden or plastic spatula to scrape the cooking surface for removing cooked food residues or grease.
4. Then scrub the cooking surface with the help of a damp sponge and little dishwashing detergents. Then again clean the cooking surface with the help of a clean damp cloth.
5. The Hamilton Panini Press Gill comes with the non-stick cooking surface so do not use an abrasive cleaner or steel wool to clean cooking surface. It may be damage the non-stick coating over the cooking surface area.
6. Take a clean damp cloth to clean the outside surface of the Hamilton Panini Press Grill.
7. After finishing the cleaning process you can store the Hamilton Panini Press at upright at hinge side to save the kitchen top space.
8. Now your Hamilton Beach Electric Panini Press Grill is ready for next use.

Chapter 2: Breakfast Panini's

Scramble Egg Breakfast Panini

Preparation Time: 10 minutes
Cooking Time: 15 minutes
Serve: 4

Ingredients:

- 4 eggs
- 1 tbsp olive oil
- 1/4 cup salsa
- 4 cheddar cheese slices
- 8 French bread slices
- 1 mango, peel & sliced thinly

Directions:

1. Spray pan with cooking spray and heat over medium heat.
2. In a bowl, whisk eggs. Pour eggs into the hot pan and cook until set and stir to scramble.
3. Preheat Panini press.
4. Add 1/4 scrambled eggs on top of 4 bread slices then add mango slices, salsa, and other bread slices.
5. Brush the outsides of the bread with oil and place on a hot Panini press.
6. Close Panini press and cook until golden brown.
7. Serve and enjoy.

Nutritional Value (Amount per Serving):

- Calories 446
- Fat 18.7 g
- Carbohydrates 50.4 g
- Sugar 14.1 g
- Protein 21 g
- Cholesterol 193 mg

Cream Cheese Apple Panini

Preparation Time: 10 minutes
Cooking Time: 15 minutes
Serve: 2

Ingredients:

- 1 egg
- 4 whole-wheat bread slices
- 4 tbsp cream cheese, softened
- 1/4 cup milk
- 1 egg whites
- 1 apple, thinly sliced

1. Add apple slices into the microwave-safe dish and microwave for 4-5 minutes.
2. In a large bowl, whip eggs with milk.
3. Preheat Panini press.
4. Spread 1 tablespoon of cream cheese on each bread slice.
5. Take 2 bread slices and stuff the cream cheese sides with sliced apples to make a sandwich.
6. Dip sandwiches in egg and place on a hot Panini press.
7. Close Panini press and cook for 4-5 minutes or until golden brown.
8. Serve and enjoy.

Nutritional Value (Amount per Serving):

- Calories 321
- Fat 11.9 g
- Carbohydrates 40.8 g
- Sugar 16.4 g
- Protein 14.6 g
- Cholesterol 106 mg

Peanut Butter Pumpkin Panini

Preparation Time: 10 minutes
Cooking Time: 10 minutes
Serve: 2

Ingredients:

- 4 bread slices
- 1 banana, cut into slices
- 1 tsp ground cinnamon
- 1/2 tsp pumpkin pie spice
- 2 tbsp maple syrup
- 1/2 cup peanut butter
- 1/2 cup can pumpkin puree

Directions:

1. In a small bowl, mix pumpkin puree, pumpkin pie spice, maple syrup, and peanut butter.
2. Spread 1 tablespoon pumpkin puree mixture on each bread slice.
3. Take 2 bread slices and top with banana slices. Top each with 2nd bread slice to make sandwiches.
4. Preheat Panini press.
5. Place sandwiches on a hot Panini press.
6. Close Panini press and cook for 4-5 minutes or until golden brown.
7. Serve and enjoy.

Nutritional Value (Amount per Serving):

- Calories 546
- Fat 33.3 g
- Carbohydrates 52.4 g
- Sugar 27 g
- Protein 18.5 g
- Cholesterol 0 mg

Tomato Bacon Egg Panini

Preparation Time: 10 minutes
Cooking Time: 15 minutes
Serve: 2

Ingredients:

- 2 eggs
- 2 Swiss cheese slices
- 4 tomato slices
- 4 bacon slices, cooked
- 4 whole-wheat bread slices
- 2 tbsp butter
- 2 tbsp water
- Pepper
- Salt

Directions:

1. Spray pan with cooking spray and heat over medium heat.
2. In a bowl, whisk eggs with water, pepper, and salt.
3. Pour eggs into the hot pan and cook until set and stir to scramble.
4. Preheat Panini press.
5. Spread butter on one side of each bread slice.
6. Take 2 bread slices and top with bacon, tomato slices, egg scramble, and cheese then cover with remaining bread. Make sure buttered side up.
7. Place sandwiches on a hot Panini press.
8. Close Panini press and cook for 4-5 minutes or until cheese is melted.
9. Serve and enjoy.

Nutritional Value (Amount per Serving):

- Calories 621
- Fat 41.5 g
- Carbohydrates 26.7 g
- Sugar 4.6 g
- Protein 34.8 g
- Cholesterol 262 mg

Arugula Bacon Cheese Panini

Preparation Time: 10 minutes
Cooking Time: 5 minutes
Serve: 1

Ingredients:

- 2 bread slices
- 1/4 cup arugula
- 1 fried egg
- 2 bacon slices, cooked
- 3 tbsp cheddar cheese, grated

Directions:

1. Take one bread slice and sprinkle with cheese then top with bacon slices, egg, and arugula. Cover with remaining bread slice.
2. Preheat Panini press.
3. Spray sandwich with cooking spray and place on a hot Panini press.
4. Close Panini press and cook for 4-5 minutes or until golden brown.
5. Serve and enjoy.

Nutritional Value (Amount per Serving):

- Calories 340
- Fat 23.5 g
- Carbohydrates 10.1 g
- Sugar 1 g
- Protein 20.9 g
- Cholesterol 64 mg

Tomato Bacon Cheddar Panini

Preparation Time: 10 minutes
Cooking Time: 15 minutes
Serve: 4

Ingredients:

- 8 bread slices
- 4 tomato slices
- 8 bacon slices, cooked
- 10 oz cheddar cheese, shredded
- 2 tbsp butter, melted

Directions:

1. Brush butter on one side of each bread slice.
2. Take 4 bread slices and sprinkle with 2 tablespoons of cheddar cheese then top with bacon, tomato. Sprinkle remaining cheese on top.
3. Cover with remaining bread slice. Make sure buttered side up.
4. Preheat Panini press.
5. Place 2 sandwiches on a hot Panini press.
6. Close Panini press and cook for 5-6 minutes or until golden brown.
7. Serve and enjoy.

Nutritional Value (Amount per Serving):

- Calories 593
- Fat 45.8 g
- Carbohydrates 11.1 g
- Sugar 1.5 g
- Protein 33.3 g
- Cholesterol 131 mg

Easy Banana Peanut Butter Panini

Preparation Time: 10 minutes
Cooking Time: 5 minutes
Serve: 1

Ingredients:

- 2 bread slices
- 1/4 tsp ground cinnamon
- 1 tbsp honey
- 1/2 banana, cut into slices
- 4 tbsp peanut butter

Directions:

1. Take one bread slice and spread with butter then top with banana slices. Drizzle with honey. Sprinkle with cinnamon.
2. Cover with remaining bread.
3. Preheat Panini press.
4. Spray sandwich with cooking spray and place on a hot Panini press.
5. Close Panini press and cook for 4-5 minutes or until golden brown.
6. Serve and enjoy.

Nutritional Value (Amount per Serving):

- Calories 542
- Fat 33 g
- Carbohydrates 53 g
- Sugar 31.3 g
- Protein 18.1 g
- Cholesterol 0 mg

Italian Breakfast Panini

Preparation Time: 10 minutes
Cooking Time: 5 minutes
Serve: 1

Ingredients:

- 1 flatbread
- 3 basil leaves
- 1 tomato, sliced
- 1 oz mozzarella cheese, sliced
- 2 eggs, scrambled

Directions:

1. Preheat Panini press.
2. Fold flatbread and stuff with scrambled egg, cheese, tomato slices, and basil.
3. Spray sandwich with cooking spray and place on a hot Panini press.
4. Close Panini press and cook for 4-5 minutes or until golden brown.
5. Serve and enjoy.

Nutritional Value (Amount per Serving):

- Calories 327
- Fat 15.9 g
- Carbohydrates 25.1 g
- Sugar 3.3 g
- Protein 22.7 g
- Cholesterol 342 mg

Delicious Egg Prosciutto Panini

Preparation Time: 10 minutes
Cooking Time: 15 minutes
Serve: 4

Ingredients:

- 3 eggs
- 2 egg whites
- 8 tsp butter, melted
- 1/2 cup cheddar cheese, shredded
- 8 prosciutto slices
- 8 bread slices
- 1 tbsp maple syrup
- 1 tbsp Dijon mustard
- 6 tbsp milk

Directions:

1. In a small bowl, whisk eggs, milk, and egg whites.
2. Spray pan with cooking spray and heat over medium heat.
3. Pour eggs into the hot pan and cook until set and stir to scramble.
4. Brush butter on one side of each bread slice.
5. Mix together maple syrup and mustard and spread over 4 bread slices then top with egg scramble, prosciutto, and cheese.
6. Cover with remaining bread slice. Make sure buttered side up.
7. Preheat Panini press.
8. Place 2 sandwiches on a hot Panini press.
9. Close Panini press and cook for 3-4 minutes or until golden brown.
10. Serve and enjoy.

Nutritional Value (Amount per Serving):

- Calories 502
- Fat 26.2 g
- Carbohydrates 16.9 g
- Sugar 5.3 g

- Protein 47.4 g
- Cholesterol 250 mg

Apple Gruyere Panini

Preparation Time: 10 minutes
Cooking Time: 5 minutes
Serve: 2

Ingredients:

- 4 whole-grain bread slices
- 1/2 apple, cored & sliced
- 4 oz Gruyere cheese, sliced
- 2 tbsp fig jam
- 2 tbsp butter, melted

Directions:

1. Brush butter on one side of each bread slice.
2. Preheat Panini press.
3. Take two bread slices and spread with fig jam then top with apple slices and cheese. Cover with remaining bread slice. Make sure buttered side up.
4. Place sandwiches on a hot Panini press.
5. Close Panini press and cook for 4-5 minutes or until golden brown.
6. Serve and enjoy.

Nutritional Value (Amount per Serving):

- Calories 543
- Fat 32.1 g
- Carbohydrates 44.2 g
- Sugar 21.3 g
- Protein 23.5 g
- Cholesterol 93 mg

Blueberry Panini

Preparation Time: 10 minutes
Cooking Time: 5 minutes
Serve: 1

Ingredients:

- 2 bread slices
- 1/4 cup blueberries
- 1 tbsp vanilla yogurt

Directions:

1. Preheat Panini press.

2. Take one bread slice and spread with yogurt then top with blueberries. Cover with remaining bread.
3. Place sandwiches on a hot Panini press.
4. Close Panini press and cook for 4-5 minutes or until golden brown.
5. Serve and enjoy.

Nutritional Value (Amount per Serving):

- Calories 80
- Fat 0.9 g
- Carbohydrates 15.4 g
- Sugar 5.5 g
- Protein 2.5 g
- Cholesterol 1 mg

Breakfast Apple Panini

Preparation Time: 10 minutes
Cooking Time: 5 minutes
Serve: 2

Ingredients:

- 4 bread slices
- 1 cup gruyere cheese, shredded
- 1 cup cheddar cheese, shredded
- 2 tsp thyme leaves
- 2 apples, cored and sliced thinly
- 1 tbsp honey
- 2 tbsp Dijon mustard
- 2 tbsp butter, melted

Directions:

1. Preheat Panini press.
2. Brush butter on one side of each bread slice.
3. In a small bowl, whisk honey and mustard.
4. Take 2 bread slices and spread with the honey mixture then top with apple slices, thyme, and cheese. Cover with remaining bread.
5. Place sandwiches on a hot Panini press.
6. Close Panini press and cook for 5 minutes or until golden brown.
7. Serve and enjoy.

Nutritional Value (Amount per Serving):

- Calories 762
- Fat 49.4 g
- Carbohydrates 51 g
- Sugar 33.2 g
- Protein 33.1 g
- Cholesterol 149 mg

Apple Ham Cheese Panini

Preparation Time: 10 minutes
Cooking Time: 10 minutes
Serve: 4

Ingredients:

- 8 bread slices
- 8 ham slices
- 2 cups Gruyere cheese, shredded
- 1/2 cup whole-grain mustard
- 1 tbsp thyme, chopped
- 2 apples, peel, cored, & sliced thinly
- 2 tbsp butter, melted

Directions:

1. Melt butter in a pan over medium heat.
2. Add apple slices and thyme and cook for 4 minutes. Remove from heat and let it cool.
3. Preheat Panini press.
4. Spread each bread slice with mustard.
5. Sprinkle 1/4 cup of cheese on 4 bread slices and top each with 2 ham slices. Add apple mixture on top of the ham and sprinkle with remaining cheese.
6. Cover with remaining bread slices.
7. Place 2 sandwiches on a hot Panini press.
8. Close Panini press and cook for 5-6 minutes or until golden brown.
9. Serve and enjoy.

Nutritional Value (Amount per Serving):

- Calories 493
- Fat 29.9 g
- Carbohydrates 29.3 g
- Sugar 12.6 g
- Protein 27.2 g
- Cholesterol 107 mg

Almond Butter Banana Panini

Preparation Time: 10 minutes
Cooking Time: 5 minutes
Serve: 1

Ingredients:

- 2 whole-wheat bread slices
- 2 tbsp butter, softened
- 1 banana, sliced
- 1 tbsp almond butter

Directions:

1. Preheat Panini press.
2. Spread each bread slice with butter.
3. Take 1 bread slice and spread with almond butter then top with banana slices. Cover with remaining bread.
4. Place sandwich on a hot Panini press.
5. Close Panini press and cook for 5 minutes or until golden brown.
6. Serve and enjoy.

Nutritional Value (Amount per Serving):

- Calories 545
- Fat 34.3 g
- Carbohydrates 53.1 g
- Sugar 18.3 g
- Protein 12.2 g
- Cholesterol 61 mg

Apple Almond Butter Panini

Preparation Time: 10 minutes
Cooking Time: 5 minutes
Serve: 2

Ingredients:

- 4 bread slices
- 2 tbsp butter, softened
- 8 green apple slices
- 1/4 cup almond butter
- 1/4 cup honey

Directions:

1. Spread each bread slice with butter.
2. In a small bowl, mix honey and almond butter.
3. Take 2 bread slices and spread with honey almond butter mixture then top with apple slices. Cover with remaining bread.
4. Place sandwiches on a hot Panini press.
5. Close Panini press and cook for 5 minutes or until golden brown.
6. Serve and enjoy.

Nutritional Value (Amount per Serving):

- Calories 294
- Fat 13.2 g
- Carbohydrates 45.2 g
- Sugar 36.3 g
- Protein 2.1 g
- Cholesterol 31 mg

Chapter 3: Vegetable Panini's

Tomato Avocado Cheddar Panini

Preparation Time: 10 minutes
Cooking Time: 5 minutes
Serve: 2

Ingredients:

- 4 bread slices
- 1 tbsp butter
- 1 tomato, sliced
- 4 Colby jack cheese slices
- 1 tsp lemon juice
- 1 avocado, mashed
- 1/2 tsp salt

Directions:

1. In a small bowl, mix avocado, lemon juice, and salt.
2. Preheat Panini press.
3. Spread butter on one side of each bread slice.
4. Take 2 bread slices and spread with the avocado mixture then top with tomato and cheese.
5. Cover with remaining bread slices. Make sure buttered side up.
6. Place sandwiches on a hot Panini press.
7. Close Panini press and cook for 4-5 minutes or until golden brown.
8. Serve and enjoy.

Nutritional Value (Amount per Serving):

- Calories 530
- Fat 44 g
- Carbohydrates 21 g
- Sugar 2.2 g
- Protein 15.6 g
- Cholesterol 65 mg

Caprese Panini

Preparation Time: 10 minutes
Cooking Time: 5 minutes
Serve: 2

Ingredients:

- 4 bread slices
- 4 tbsp basil pesto
- 4 oz mozzarella cheese
- 1 avocado, sliced

- 2 small tomatoes, sliced
- 1 tbsp butter

Directions:

1. Preheat Panini press.
2. Spread butter on one side of each bread slice.
3. Take 2 bread slices and spread with pesto then top with tomatoes, avocado, and cheese.
4. Cover with remaining bread slices. Make sure buttered side up.
5. Place sandwiches on a hot Panini press.
6. Close Panini press and cook for 4-5 minutes or until golden brown.
7. Serve and enjoy.

Nutritional Value (Amount per Serving):

- Calories 481
- Fat 36.2 g
- Carbohydrates 23.4 g
- Sugar 3.7 g
- Protein 20.3 g
- Cholesterol 45 mg

Veggie Avocado Panini

Preparation Time: 10 minutes
Cooking Time: 10 minutes
Serve: 4

Ingredients:

- 8 whole-wheat bread slices
- 2 avocados
- 2 cups kale, chopped
- 1 cup cherry tomatoes
- 8 oz baby mushrooms, sliced
- 1 shallot, minced
- 1 1/2 tbsp butter
- Salt

Directions:

1. Melt butter in a pan over medium-high heat.
2. Add shallot and sauté until translucent.
3. Add mushrooms and sauté until lightly browned.
4. Add kale and tomatoes and cook until kale is wilted. Remove pan from heat and season with salt.
5. In a small bowl, mash the avocados using a fork.
6. Take 4 bread slices and spread with mashed avocado then top sautéed vegetables.
7. Cover with remaining bread slices.
8. Place 2 sandwiches on a hot Panini press.
9. Close Panini press and cook for 4-5 minutes or until golden brown.

10. Serve and enjoy.

Nutritional Value (Amount per Serving):

- Calories 424
- Fat 25.9 g
- Carbohydrates 39.1 g
- Sugar 4.8 g
- Protein 12.3 g
- Cholesterol 11 mg

Avocado Chickpeas Panini

Preparation Time: 10 minutes
Cooking Time: 10 minutes
Serve: 4

Ingredients:

- 8 bread slices
- 1 cup baby spinach
- 1 tomato, sliced
- 1 tbsp fresh lemon juice
- 2 tbsp onion, diced
- 1/4 cup basil pesto
- 1 avocado
- 15 oz can chickpeas, drained & rinsed
- 2 tbsp butter
- Salt

Directions:

1. In a bowl, mash avocado and chickpeas using a potato masher. Add pesto, onion, lemon juice, and salt and mix well.
2. Preheat Panini press.
3. Spread butter on one side of each bread slice.
4. Take 4 bread slices and spread with the avocado mixture then top with tomatoes and spinach.
5. Cover with remaining bread slices. Make sure buttered side up.
6. Place 2 sandwiches on a hot Panini press.
7. Close Panini press and cook for 4-5 minutes or until golden brown.
8. Serve and enjoy.

Nutritional Value (Amount per Serving):

- Calories 336
- Fat 17.5 g
- Carbohydrates 38.9 g
- Sugar 1.8 g
- Protein 8.1 g
- Cholesterol 15 mg

Pesto Avocado Cheese Panini

Preparation Time: 10 minutes
Cooking Time: 5 minutes
Serve: 1

Ingredients:

- 2 bread slices
- 4 tsp mayonnaise
- 1/2 avocado, sliced
- 3 mozzarella cheese slices
- 2 tbsp pesto

Directions:

1. Preheat Panini press.
2. Spread mayonnaise on one side of each bread slice.
3. Take 1 bread slice and spread with pesto then top with avocado and mozzarella cheese slices.
4. Cover with remaining bread slice. Make sure mayo side up.
5. Place sandwich on a hot Panini press.
6. Close Panini press and cook for 4-5 minutes or until golden brown.
7. Serve and enjoy.

Nutritional Value (Amount per Serving):

- Calories 704
- Fat 54.7 g
- Carbohydrates 27.4 g
- Sugar 4.5 g
- Protein 30.5 g
- Cholesterol 58 mg

Artichoke Spinach Panini

Preparation Time: 10 minutes
Cooking Time: 10 minutes
Serve: 4

Ingredients:

- 8 bread slices
- 1 cup baby spinach
- 8 oz mozzarella cheese, shredded
- 12 oz grilled chicken strips
- 6.5 oz marinated artichoke hearts, chopped
- 1/4 cup cream cheese spread
- 2 tbsp butter

Directions:

1. Preheat Panini press.
2. Spread butter on one side of each bread slice.
3. Take 4 bread slices and spread with cream cheese spread then top with artichoke hearts, chicken strips, spinach, and mozzarella cheese.
4. Cover with remaining bread slices. Make sure buttered side up.
5. Place 2 sandwiches on a hot Panini press.
6. Close Panini press and cook for 4-5 minutes or until golden brown.
7. Serve and enjoy.

Nutritional Value (Amount per Serving):

- Calories 704
- Fat 54.7 g
- Carbohydrates 27.4 g
- Sugar 4.5 g
- Protein 30.5 g
- Cholesterol 58 mg

Spinach Tomato Panini

Preparation Time: 10 minutes
Cooking Time: 5 minutes
Serve: 1

Ingredients:

- 2 bread slices
- 1 cheese slice
- 1 cup frozen spinach, thawed & drained
- 1/2 tomato, sliced
- 1 tbsp tomato pesto
- 1 tbsp mayonnaise
- 2 tsp butter

Directions:

1. Preheat Panini press.
2. Spread butter on one side of each bread slice.
3. In a small bowl, mix together mayonnaise and tomato pesto.
4. Take 1 bread slice and spread with mayonnaise mixture then top with tomato, spinach, and cheese slice.
5. Cover with remaining bread slice. Make sure buttered side up.
6. Place sandwich on a hot Panini press.
7. Close Panini press and cook for 4-5 minutes or until golden brown.
8. Serve and enjoy.

Nutritional Value (Amount per Serving):

- Calories 583
- Fat 50.5 g
- Carbohydrates 20.5 g
- Sugar 6.8 g

- Protein 13.8 g
- Cholesterol 53 mg

Potato Spinach Panini

Preparation Time: 10 minutes
Cooking Time: 5 minutes
Serve: 2

Ingredients:

- 4 bread slices
- 1/2 cup spinach, cooked
- 1/2 cup mashed potatoes
- 2 tbsp mayonnaise
- 1 tbsp butter

Directions:

1. Preheat Panini press.
2. Spread butter on one side of each bread slice.
3. Take 2 bread slices and spread with mayonnaise then top with mashed potatoes and spinach.
4. Cover with remaining bread slices. Make sure buttered side up.
5. Place sandwiches on a hot Panini press.
6. Close Panini press and cook for 4-5 minutes or until golden brown.
7. Serve and enjoy.

Nutritional Value (Amount per Serving):

- Calories 208
- Fat 12 g
- Carbohydrates 22.7 g
- Sugar 1.8 g
- Protein 3.2 g
- Cholesterol 20 mg

Tomato Zucchini Panini

Preparation Time: 10 minutes
Cooking Time: 5 minutes
Serve: 2

Ingredients:

- 4 bread slices
- 1 tbsp butter
- 1/2 cup mozzarella cheese, shredded
- 1 tomato, sliced
- 1 zucchini, sliced

Directions:

1. Preheat Panini press.
2. Spread butter on one side of each bread slice.
3. Take 2 bread slices and top with zucchini, tomato, and cheese.
4. Cover with remaining bread slices. Make sure buttered side up.
5. Place sandwiches on a hot Panini press.
6. Close Panini press and cook for 4-5 minutes or until golden brown.
7. Serve and enjoy.

Nutritional Value (Amount per Serving):

- Calories 140
- Fat 7.8 g
- Carbohydrates 13.9 g
- Sugar 3.3 g
- Protein 4.9 g
- Cholesterol 19 mg

Pear Spinach Feta Panini

Preparation Time: 10 minutes
Cooking Time: 5 minutes
Serve: 2

Ingredients:

- 4 bread slices
- 1 tbsp vinegar
- 1 tbsp walnuts, toasted
- 1 tbsp fresh sage, chopped
- 1/2 cup baby spinach
- 2 oz feta cheese, crumbled
- 1 ripe pear, sliced thinly
- 2 tbsp cream cheese, softened
- 1 tbsp butter

Directions:

1. Preheat Panini press.
2. Spread butter on one side of each bread slice.
3. Take 2 bread slices and spread with cream cheese then top with pear, spinach, feta cheese, sage, and walnuts. Drizzle with vinegar.
4. Cover with remaining bread slices. Make sure buttered side up.
5. Place sandwiches on a hot Panini press.
6. Close Panini press and cook for 4-5 minutes or until golden brown.
7. Serve and enjoy.

Nutritional Value (Amount per Serving):

- Calories 279
- Fat 18.4 g
- Carbohydrates 22.5 g
- Sugar 8.9 g

- Protein 7.7 g
- Cholesterol 52 mg

Tasty Avocado Spinach Panini

Preparation Time: 10 minutes
Cooking Time: 5 minutes
Serve: 1

Ingredients:

- 2 bread slices
- 6 spinach leaves
- 1/2 avocado, chopped
- 2 pepper jack cheese slices
- 2 tsp butter

Directions:

1. Preheat Panini press.
2. Spread butter on one side of each bread slice.
3. Take 1 bread slice and top with avocado, spinach, and cheese.
4. Cover with remaining bread slice. Make sure buttered side up.
5. Place sandwich on a hot Panini press.
6. Close Panini press and cook for 4-5 minutes or until golden brown.
7. Serve and enjoy.

Nutritional Value (Amount per Serving):

- Calories 554
- Fat 46 g
- Carbohydrates 19.9 g
- Sugar 1.5 g
- Protein 19.1 g
- Cholesterol 80 mg

Basil Tomato Panini

Preparation Time: 10 minutes
Cooking Time: 5 minutes
Serve: 1

Ingredients:

- 2 whole-wheat bread slices
- 1 tbsp butter
- 8 fresh basil leaves
- 1 onion sliced
- 1 tomato, sliced
- 1/2 cup mozzarella cheese, shredded

Directions:

1. Preheat Panini press.

2. Spread butter on one side of each bread slice.
3. Take 1 bread slice and top with tomato, onion, basil, and cheese.
4. Cover with remaining bread slice. Make sure buttered side up.
5. Place sandwich on a hot Panini press.
6. Close Panini press and cook for 4-5 minutes or until golden brown.
7. Serve and enjoy.

Nutritional Value (Amount per Serving):

- Calories 296
- Fat 16.1 g
- Carbohydrates 27 g
- Sugar 5.2 g
- Protein 12.2 g
- Cholesterol 38 mg

Corn Zucchini Cheese Panini

Preparation Time: 10 minutes
Cooking Time: 10 minutes
Serve: 4

Ingredients:

- 8 bread slices
- 1 cup pepper jack cheese, shredded
- 2 tbsp butter
- 1 small zucchini, sliced
- 1 ear corn, kernels removed
- 1 garlic clove, minced
- 1 tbsp olive oil
- Pepper
- Salt

Directions:

1. Heat oil in a pan over medium-high heat.
2. Add garlic and cook for 15 seconds. Add zucchini and corn and cook for 3 minutes. Season with pepper and salt.
3. Remove pan from heat.
4. Preheat Panini press.
5. Spread butter on one side of each bread slice.
6. Take 4 bread slices and top with vegetable mixture and cheese.
7. Cover with remaining bread slices. Make sure buttered side up.
8. Place 2 sandwiches on a hot Panini press.
9. Close Panini press and cook for 5 minutes or until golden brown.
10. Serve and enjoy.

Nutritional Value (Amount per Serving):

- Calories 195
- Fat 12.6 g

- Carbohydrates 17.6 g
- Sugar 2.6 g
- Protein 4.9 g
- Cholesterol 23 mg

Pesto Panini

Preparation Time: 10 minutes
Cooking Time: 5 minutes
Serve: 2

Ingredients:

- 4 bread slices
- 2/3 cup mozzarella cheese, shredded
- 1/4 cup basil leaves, chopped
- 1/2 tomato, sliced
- 1 garlic clove, minced
- 1 tsp tomato paste
- 2 tbsp olives, chopped
- 3 tbsp pesto
- 1 tbsp butter

Directions:

1. Preheat Panini press.
2. Spread butter on one side of each bread slice.
3. In a small bowl, mix pesto, tomato paste, garlic, and basil.
4. Take 2 bread slices and spread with pesto mixture and top with tomato, olives, and cheese.
5. Cover with remaining bread slices. Make sure buttered side up.
6. Place sandwiches on a hot Panini press.
7. Close Panini press and cook for 5 minutes or until golden brown.
8. Serve and enjoy.

Nutritional Value (Amount per Serving):

- Calories 244
- Fat 18.7 g
- Carbohydrates 13.2 g
- Sugar 3.1 g
- Protein 6.9 g
- Cholesterol 26 mg

Sun-dried Tomato Spinach Panini

Preparation Time: 10 minutes
Cooking Time: 5 minutes
Serve: 2

Ingredients:

- 4 bread slices
- 1/4 cup parmesan cheese, shaved

- 1/4 cup sun-dried tomatoes, sliced
- 1 cup baby spinach
- 1 tbsp butter
- 1/4 tsp Italian seasoning
- 1/4 cup ricotta cheese
- 1/4 cup goat cheese

Directions:

1. Preheat Panini press.
2. Spread butter on one side of each bread slice.
3. In a small bowl, mix ricotta cheese, Italian seasoning, and goat cheese.
4. Take 2 bread slices and spread with cheese mixture and top with spinach, tomatoes, and parmesan cheese.
5. Cover with remaining bread slices. Make sure buttered side up.
6. Place sandwiches on a hot Panini press.
7. Close Panini press and cook for 5 minutes or until golden brown.
8. Serve and enjoy.

Nutritional Value (Amount per Serving):

- Calories 203
- Fat 12.8 g
- Carbohydrates 12.7 g
- Sugar 1.7 g
- Protein 10.3 g
- Cholesterol 37 mg

Pesto Sun-dried Tomato Panini

Preparation Time: 10 minutes
Cooking Time: 5 minutes
Serve: 1

Ingredients:

- 2 bread slices
- 2 mozzarella cheese slices
- 3 tomato slices
- 2 tsp pine nuts
- 2 tbsp sun-dried tomato pesto
- 2 tsp butter

Directions:

1. Preheat Panini press.
2. Spread butter on one side of each bread slice.
3. Take 1 bread slice and spread with tomato pesto and top with pine nuts, tomato slices, and cheese.
4. Cover with remaining bread slice. Make sure buttered side up.
5. Place sandwich on a hot Panini press.
6. Close Panini press and cook for 5 minutes or until golden brown.
7. Serve and enjoy.

Nutritional Value (Amount per Serving):

- Calories 340
- Fat 22.6 g
- Carbohydrates 14.9 g
- Sugar 3 g
- Protein 20.8 g
- Cholesterol 52 mg

Arugula Eggplant Panini

Preparation Time: 10 minutes
Cooking Time: 10 minutes
Serve: 4

Ingredients:

- 8 bread slices
- 8 mozzarella cheese slices
- 2 cups arugula leaves
- 4 eggplant slices
- 1 tbsp olive oil
- 2 tbsp butter

Directions:

1. Brush eggplant slices with oil and grill for 4 minutes.
2. Preheat Panini press.
3. Spread butter on one side of each bread slice.
4. Take 4 bread slices and top with eggplant slices, arugula, and cheese.
5. Cover with remaining bread slices. Make sure buttered side up.
6. Place 2 sandwiches on a hot Panini press.
7. Close Panini press and cook for 5 minutes or until golden brown.
8. Serve and enjoy.

Nutritional Value (Amount per Serving):

- Calories 406
- Fat 20.7 g
- Carbohydrates 38.4 g
- Sugar 14.7 g
- Protein 22.2 g
- Cholesterol 45 mg

Eggplant Cheese Panini

Preparation Time: 10 minutes
Cooking Time: 10 minutes
Serve: 4

Ingredients:

- 8 bread slices
- 8 mozzarella cheese slices

- 1 cup marinara sauce
- 1 eggplant, cut into 1/4-inch slices
- 2 tbsp olive oil
- 2 tbsp butter

Directions:

1. Heat oil in a pan over medium heat. Add eggplant slices and sauté well.
2. Preheat Panini press.
3. Spread butter on one side of each bread slice.
4. Take 4 bread slices and spread with marinara sauce and top with eggplant slices and cheese.
5. Cover with remaining bread slices. Make sure buttered side up.
6. Place 2 sandwiches on a hot Panini press.
7. Close Panini press and cook for 5 minutes or until golden brown.
8. Serve and enjoy.

Nutritional Value (Amount per Serving):

- Calories 402
- Fat 25.2 g
- Carbohydrates 26.4 g
- Sugar 9.8 g
- Protein 19.7 g
- Cholesterol 47 mg

Vegetable Herb Panini

Preparation Time: 10 minutes
Cooking Time: 5 minutes
Serve: 2

Ingredients:

- 4 Tuscan bread slices
- 2 oz mozzarella cheese
- 1 tbsp fresh basil, chopped
- 2 garlic cloves, minced
- 1/4 cup honey mustard
- 2 tbsp olive oil
- 1 red pepper, quartered
- 1 small zucchini, cut into slices
- 1 small eggplant, cut into slices
- Pepper
- Salt

Directions:

1. Preheat the oven to 425 F.
2. Arrange veggies on a baking sheet and drizzle with oil. Season with pepper and salt and bake in a preheated oven for 10 minutes.
3. In a small bowl, mix basil, garlic, and honey mustard.
4. Preheat Panini press.

5. Take 2 bread slices and spread with basil mixture and top with baked vegetables and cheese.
6. Cover with remaining bread slices.
7. Place sandwiches on a hot Panini press.
8. Close Panini press and cook for 5 minutes or until golden brown.
9. Serve and enjoy.

Nutritional Value (Amount per Serving):

- Calories 351
- Fat 19.7 g
- Carbohydrates 34 g
- Sugar 16.9 g
- Protein 11.8 g
- Cholesterol 15 mg

Greek Vegetable Panini

Preparation Time: 10 minutes
Cooking Time: 5 minutes
Serve: 2

Ingredients:

- 4 whole-grain bread slices
- 2 roasted bell pepper, cut into strips
- 4 tsp Italian salad dressing
- 2 small zucchini, cut into slices
- 2/3 cup mushrooms, sliced
- 2/3 cup mozzarella cheese, shredded
- 2 tomato, sliced
- 1 tbsp butter

Directions:

1. Preheat Panini press.
2. Spread butter on one side of each bread slice.
3. Take 2 bread slices and top with tomato, mushrooms, zucchini, bell pepper, and cheese. Drizzle with dressing.
4. Cover with remaining bread slices. Make sure buttered side up.
5. Place sandwiches on a hot Panini press.
6. Close Panini press and cook for 5 minutes or until golden brown.
7. Serve and enjoy.

Nutritional Value (Amount per Serving):

- Calories 321
- Fat 15 g
- Carbohydrates 40.1 g
- Sugar 9.3 g
- Protein 12.1 g
- Cholesterol 27 mg

Chapter 4: Poultry Panini's

Delicious Panera Frontega Chicken Panini

Preparation Time: 10 minutes
Cooking Time: 10 minutes
Serve: 2

Ingredients:

- 4 bread slices
- 12 basil leaves, chopped
- 1/2 small onion, sliced
- 1 tomato, sliced
- 8 oz mozzarella ball, sliced
- 2 chicken breasts, cooked & shredded
- 1 chipotle pepper in adobo sauce
- 1/4 cup mayonnaise
- 1 tbsp butter

Directions:

1. Add chipotle pepper and mayonnaise in a blender and blend until smooth.
2. Preheat Panini press.
3. Spread butter on one side of each bread slice.
4. Take 2 bread slices and spread with mayo mixture and top with chicken, tomato, onion, cheese, and basil.
5. Cover with remaining bread slices. Make sure buttered side up.
6. Place sandwiches on a hot Panini press.
7. Close Panini press and cook for 5 minutes or until golden brown.
8. Serve and enjoy.

Nutritional Value (Amount per Serving):

- Calories 828
- Fat 51.4 g
- Carbohydrates 19.1 g
- Sugar 4.2 g
- Protein 71.5 g
- Cholesterol 234 mg

Cheesy Chicken Panini

Preparation Time: 10 minutes
Cooking Time: 5 minutes
Serve: 1

Ingredients:

- 2 whole-wheat bread slices
- 1/4 tsp oregano

- 2 tbsp marinara sauce
- 2 1/2 oz chicken breast, cooked & shredded
- 1/2 cup mozzarella cheese, shredded
- 1 garlic clove, minced
- 2 tbsp mushrooms, chopped
- 2 tbsp onions, chopped
- 1 tbsp olive oil

Directions:

1. Heat oil in a pan over medium heat.
2. Add garlic, mushrooms, and onions, and sauté until onion is softened.
3. Preheat Panini press.
4. Take 1 bread slice and spread with marinara sauce and top with chicken, oregano, sautéed vegetables, and cheese.
5. Cover with remaining bread slice.
6. Place sandwich on a hot Panini press.
7. Close Panini press and cook for 5 minutes or until golden brown.
8. Serve and enjoy.

Nutritional Value (Amount per Serving):

- Calories 422
- Fat 21.1 g
- Carbohydrates 31.3 g
- Sugar 6.9 g
- Protein 27.6 g
- Cholesterol 53 mg

Turkey Panini

Preparation Time: 10 minutes
Cooking Time: 5 minutes
Serve: 1

Ingredients:

- 2 bread slices
- 1 tbsp fresh thyme leaves
- 1 provolone cheese slice
- 2 tbsp cranberry sauce
- 3 oz turkey breast, cooked and shredded
- 1 tbsp mayonnaise

Directions:

1. Preheat Panini press.
2. Spread mayo on one side of each bread slice.
3. Take 1 bread slice and top with turkey, thyme, cranberry sauce, and cheese.
4. Cover with remaining bread slice. Make sure mayo side up.
5. Place sandwich on a hot Panini press.
6. Close Panini press and cook for 5 minutes or until golden brown.

7. Serve and enjoy.

Nutritional Value (Amount per Serving):

- Calories 307
- Fat 14.6 g
- Carbohydrates 19.8 g
- Sugar 5.4 g
- Protein 23.4 g
- Cholesterol 60 mg

Greek Chicken Panini

Preparation Time: 10 minutes
Cooking Time: 5 minutes
Serve: 2

Ingredients:

- 1 chicken breast, cooked & shredded
- 4 bread slices
- 4 oz mozzarella cheese, shredded
- 1/2 cup roasted red peppers, sliced
- 2 onion sliced
- 2 tbsp pesto
- 1 tbsp butter

Directions:

1. Preheat Panini press.
2. Spread butter on one side of each bread slice.
3. Take 2 bread slices and spread with pesto and top with chicken, onion, red peppers, and cheese.
4. Cover with remaining bread slices. Make sure buttered side up.
5. Place sandwiches on a hot Panini press.
6. Close Panini press and cook for 5 minutes or until golden brown.
7. Serve and enjoy.

Nutritional Value (Amount per Serving):

- Calories 399
- Fat 24.2 g
- Carbohydrates 15.8 g
- Sugar 4.2 g
- Protein 30.1 g
- Cholesterol 24.2 mg

Easy Buffalo Chicken Panini

Preparation Time: 10 minutes
Cooking Time: 5 minutes
Serve: 2

Ingredients:

- 4 bread slices
- 1/4 cup blue cheese
- 4 mozzarella cheese slices
- 1/2 cup buffalo chicken sauce
- 1 chicken breast, cooked & shredded
- 1 tbsp butter

Directions:

1. Preheat Panini press.
2. Spread butter on one side of each bread slice.
3. In a bowl, mix chicken, buffalo sauce, and blue cheese.
4. Take 2 bread slices and top with chicken and cheese.
5. Cover with remaining bread slices. Make sure buttered side up.
6. Place sandwiches on a hot Panini press.
7. Close Panini press and cook for 5 minutes or until golden brown.
8. Serve and enjoy.

Nutritional Value (Amount per Serving):

- Calories 483
- Fat 30 g
- Carbohydrates 11.5 g
- Sugar 0.9 g
- Protein 40.7 g
- Cholesterol 119 mg

Spinach Pesto Chicken Panini

Preparation Time: 10 minutes
Cooking Time: 10 minutes
Serve: 4

Ingredients:

- 8 bread slices
- 8 Swiss cheese slices
- 1 cup baby spinach
- 1 1/2 cups chicken breast, cooked & shredded
- 2 tbsp pesto
- 1/2 cup mayonnaise
- 2 tbsp butter
- Pepper
- Salt

Directions:

1. Preheat Panini press.
2. Spread butter on one side of each bread slice.
3. In a bowl, mix chicken, mayonnaise, pesto, pepper, and salt.
4. Take 4 bread slices and top with chicken mixture, spinach, and cheese.
5. Cover with remaining bread slices. Make sure buttered side up.

6. Place 2 sandwiches on a hot Panini press.
7. Close Panini press and cook for 5 minutes or until golden brown.
8. Serve and enjoy.

Nutritional Value (Amount per Serving):

- Calories 504
- Fat 36 g
- Carbohydrates 19.9 g
- Sugar 3.9 g
- Protein 25.7 g
- Cholesterol 100 mg

Chicken Bacon Avocado Panini

Preparation Time: 10 minutes
Cooking Time: 5 minutes
Serve: 2

Ingredients:

- 4 bread slices
- 6 Provolone cheese slices
- 1/4 avocado, sliced
- 1/2 tomato, sliced
- 2 bacon slices, cooked
- 1/2 chicken breast, cooked & shredded
- 1 tbsp butter
- 1/4 tsp lemon juice
- 2 tsp hot sauce
- 1/3 cup mayonnaise
- Pepper
- Salt

Directions:

1. Preheat Panini press.
2. Spread butter on one side of each bread slice.
3. In a bowl, mix mayonnaise, hot sauce, lemon juice, pepper, and salt.
4. Take 2 bread slices and spread with mayo mixture and top with chicken, bacon, tomato, avocado, and cheese.
5. Cover with remaining bread slices. Make sure buttered side up.
6. Place sandwiches on a hot Panini press.
7. Close Panini press and cook for 5 minutes or until golden brown.
8. Serve and enjoy.

Nutritional Value (Amount per Serving):

- Calories 733
- Fat 55.3 g
- Carbohydrates 23.4 g
- Sugar 4.4 g
- Protein 36.3 g
- Cholesterol 120 mg

Ranch Chicken Panini

Preparation Time: 10 minutes
Cooking Time: 5 minutes
Serve: 1

Ingredients:

- 2 bread slices
- 1 tbsp butter
- 2 tomato slices
- 4 bacon slices, cooked
- 2 Havarti cheese slices
- 1 cup chicken, cooked and chopped
- 1/2 cup baby spinach
- 1 tbsp garlic ranch dressing

Directions:

1. Preheat Panini press.
2. Spread butter on one side of each bread slice.
3. Take 1 bread slice and spread with garlic ranch dressing then top with chicken, spinach, bacon, tomato, and cheese.
4. Cover with remaining bread slice. Make sure butter side up.
5. Place sandwich on a hot Panini press.
6. Close Panini press and cook for 5 minutes or until golden brown.
7. Serve and enjoy.

Nutritional Value (Amount per Serving):

- Calories 679
- Fat 43.7 g
- Carbohydrates 14.3 g
- Sugar 3.6 g
- Protein 57.2 g
- Cholesterol 199 mg

Pesto Tomato Chicken Panini

Preparation Time: 10 minutes
Cooking Time: 5 minutes
Serve: 2

Ingredients:

- 4 bread slices
- 1 tbsp butter
- 8 sun-dried tomatoes
- 1 1/2 cups mozzarella cheese, shredded
- 1/2 cup pesto
- 2 cups chicken, cooked & shredded

Directions:

1. Preheat Panini press.
2. Spread butter on one side of each bread slice.
3. In a bowl, mix pesto and chicken.
4. Take 2 bread slices and top with chicken, tomatoes, and cheese.
5. Cover with remaining bread slices. Make sure buttered side up.
6. Place sandwiches on a hot Panini press.
7. Close Panini press and cook for 5 minutes or until golden brown.
8. Serve and enjoy.

Nutritional Value (Amount per Serving):

- Calories 729
- Fat 41.3 g
- Carbohydrates 33 g
- Sugar 17.7 g
- Protein 58.3 g
- Cholesterol 149 mg

California Chicken Panini

Preparation Time: 10 minutes
Cooking Time: 5 minutes
Serve: 1

Ingredients:

- 2 bread slices
- 2 tsp mayonnaise
- 2 tbsp mozzarella cheese, grated
- 2 tbsp cheddar cheese, grated
- 1/4 lb smoked chicken, sliced
- 2 tomato slices
- 1/2 avocado, sliced
- 1 tbsp aioli

Directions:

1. Preheat Panini press.
2. Spread mayo on one side of each bread slice.
3. Take 1 bread slice and spread with aioli and top with chicken, tomato, avocado, and cheese.
4. Cover with remaining bread slice. Make sure mayo side up.
5. Place sandwich on a hot Panini press.
6. Close Panini press and cook for 5 minutes or until golden brown.
7. Serve and enjoy.

Nutritional Value (Amount per Serving):

- Calories 784
- Fat 58.7 g
- Carbohydrates 24.7 g
- Sugar 2.8 g
- Protein 43.5 g
- Cholesterol 107 mg

Spicy Turkey Panini

Preparation Time: 10 minutes
Cooking Time: 5 minutes
Serve: 2

Ingredients:

- 4 bread slices
- 8 roasted deli turkey slices
- 4 Colby jack cheese slices
- 2 tbsp spicy mustard
- 1/2 tomato, diced
- 1 tsp lime juice
- 1/2 avocado, scoop out the flesh
- 1/4 tsp salt

Directions:

1. Preheat Panini press.
2. In a bowl, mash avocado. Add lime juice, tomato, and salt and mix well.
3. Take 2 bread slices and spread with spicy mustard and top with turkey slices, avocado mixture, and cheese.
4. Cover with remaining bread slices.
5. Place sandwiches on a hot Panini press.
6. Close Panini press and cook for 5 minutes or until golden brown.
7. Serve and enjoy.

Nutritional Value (Amount per Serving):

- Calories 422
- Fat 16.8 g
- Carbohydrates 18.3 g
- Sugar 5.4 g
- Protein 44.1 g
- Cholesterol 107 mg

BLT Chicken Panini

Preparation Time: 10 minutes
Cooking Time: 5 minutes
Serve: 2

Ingredients:

- 4 bread slices
- 4 tomato slices
- 2 lettuce leaves
- 2 Swiss cheese slices
- 8 oz deli sliced roasted chicken
- 1 tbsp mayonnaise
- 4 bacon slices, cooked

Directions:

1. Preheat Panini press.
2. Spread mayo on one side of each bread slice.
3. Take 2 bread slices and top with chicken, cheese, lettuce, tomato, and bacon.
4. Cover with remaining bread slices. Make sure mayo side up.
5. Place sandwiches on a hot Panini press.
6. Close Panini press and cook for 5 minutes or until golden brown.
7. Serve and enjoy.

Nutritional Value (Amount per Serving):

- Calories 518
- Fat 29.3 g
- Carbohydrates 21.5 g
- Sugar 4.8 g
- Protein 41.5 g
- Cholesterol 69 mg

Apple Sauerkraut Chicken Panini

Preparation Time: 10 minutes
Cooking Time: 10 minutes
Serve: 4

Ingredients:

- 8 whole-wheat bread slices
- 4 Swiss cheese slices
- 12 oz chicken breast, cooked & sliced
- 1 apple, cored & sliced thinly
- 1 cup can sauerkraut
- 2 tbsp butter

Directions:

1. Preheat Panini press.
2. Spread butter on one side of each bread slice.
3. Take 4 bread slices and top with chicken, sauerkraut, apple slices, and cheese.
4. Cover with remaining bread slices. Make sure buttered side up.
5. Place 2 sandwiches on a hot Panini press.
6. Close Panini press and cook for 5 minutes or until golden brown.
7. Serve and enjoy.

Nutritional Value (Amount per Serving):

- Calories 432
- Fat 17.7 g
- Carbohydrates 34.3 g
- Sugar 11.3 g
- Protein 33 g
- Cholesterol 95 mg

Chipotle Chicken Panini

Preparation Time: 10 minutes
Cooking Time: 5 minutes
Serve: 1

Ingredients:

- 2 bread slices
- 2 tbsp ranch dressing
- 2 Chipotle gouda cheese slices
- 2 bacon slices, cooked
- 1 tomato slice
- 4 chicken breast slices
- 2 tsp butter

Directions:

1. Preheat Panini press.
2. Spread butter on one side of each bread slice.
3. Take 1 bread slice and top with chicken slices, tomato, bacon, cheese, and ranch dressing.
4. Cover with remaining bread slice. Make sure butter side up.
5. Place sandwich on a hot Panini press.
6. Close Panini press and cook for 5 minutes or until golden brown.
7. Serve and enjoy.

Nutritional Value (Amount per Serving):

- Calories 685
- Fat 42.9 g
- Carbohydrates 15.5 g
- Sugar 2.2 g
- Protein 58.3 g
- Cholesterol 182 mg

Pepperoni Chicken Panini

Preparation Time: 10 minutes
Cooking Time: 5 minutes
Serve: 1

Ingredients:

- 2 bread slices
- 1/2 tbsp parmesan cheese, grated
- 1 mozzarella cheese slice
- 6 pepperoni slices
- 1 tbsp marinara sauce
- 4 chicken strips
- 2 tsp butter

Directions:

1. Preheat Panini press.
2. Spread butter on one side of each bread slice.
3. Take 1 bread slice and top with chicken, marinara sauce, pepperoni slices, and cheese.
4. Cover with remaining bread slice. Make sure butter side up.
5. Place sandwich on a hot Panini press.
6. Close Panini press and cook for 5 minutes or until golden brown.
7. Serve and enjoy.

Nutritional Value (Amount per Serving):

- Calories 897
- Fat 45.2 g
- Carbohydrates 16.8 g
- Sugar 2.2 g
- Protein 105.2 g
- Cholesterol 320 mg

Tasty Curried Chicken Panini

Preparation Time: 10 minutes
Cooking Time: 10 minutes
Serve: 4

Ingredients:

- 8 whole-wheat bread slices
- 2 tbsp butter
- 1 cup arugula
- 1/3 cup mango chutney
- 1/4 tsp lemon zest
- 3/4 tsp curry powder
- 1/4 cup mayonnaise
- 1/4 cup celery, chopped
- 2 cups cooked chicken, cubed

Directions:

1. Preheat Panini press.
2. Spread butter on one side of each bread slice.
3. In a bowl, mix together chicken, celery, mayo, curry powder, and lemon zest.
4. Take 4 bread slices and spread with mango chutney top with chicken mixture and arugula.
5. Cover with remaining bread slices. Make sure buttered side up.
6. Place 2 sandwiches on a hot Panini press.
7. Close Panini press and cook for 5 minutes or until golden brown.
8. Serve and enjoy.

Nutritional Value (Amount per Serving):

- Calories 389
- Fat 14.8 g

- Carbohydrates 36.6 g
- Sugar 12.3 g
- Protein 28 g
- Cholesterol 73 mg

Creamy Chicken Cheese Panini

Preparation Time: 10 minutes
Cooking Time: 10 minutes
Serve: 4

Ingredients:

- 8 bread slices
- 4 cheddar cheese slices
- 1/2 cup blue cheese, crumbled
- 4 oz cream cheese
- 1/4 cup sour cream
- 1/4 cup mayonnaise
- 1 tsp hot sauce
- 1/2 tsp paprika
- 1/8 tsp cayenne pepper
- 1 tsp garlic powder
- 2 chicken breasts, cooked and shredded

Directions:

1. Preheat Panini press.
2. Spread mayo on one side of each bread slice.
3. In a bowl, mix together chicken, sour cream, hot sauce, paprika, cayenne, and garlic powder.
4. In a small bowl, mix cream cheese and blue cheese.
5. Take 4 bread slices and spread with cream cheese mixture top chicken mixture.
6. Cover with remaining bread slices. Make sure mayo side up.
7. Place 2 sandwiches on a hot Panini press.
8. Close Panini press and cook for 5 minutes or until golden brown.
9. Serve and enjoy.

Nutritional Value (Amount per Serving):

- Calories 549
- Fat 38 g
- Carbohydrates 15.4 g
- Sugar 2.3 g
- Protein 36 g
- Cholesterol 148 mg

Tasty Rotisserie Chicken Panini

Preparation Time: 10 minutes
Cooking Time: 5 minutes
Serve: 2

Ingredients:

- 4 bread slices
- 2 tbsp butter
- 4 tomato slices
- 2 onion sliced
- 2 mozzarella cheese slices
- 4 bacon slices, cooked
- 1/4 lb rotisserie chicken, sliced
- 1/4 tsp lemon zest
- 1/2 tsp peto
- 1 tsp lemon juice
- 4 tsp parmesan cheese, grated
- 3 tbsp mayonnaise

Directions:

1. In a small bowl, mix together mayonnaise, parmesan cheese, lemon juice, pesto, and lemon zest.
2. Preheat Panini press.
3. Spread butter on one side of each bread slice.
4. Take 2 bread slices and spread with mayo mixture and top with chicken, bacon, cheese, onion, and tomato.
5. Cover with remaining bread slices. Make sure butter side up.
6. Place sandwiches on a hot Panini press.
7. Close Panini press and cook for 5 minutes or until golden brown.
8. Serve and enjoy.

Nutritional Value (Amount per Serving):

- Calories 774
- Fat 52.8 g
- Carbohydrates 21.2 g
- Sugar 3.4 g
- Protein 56 g
- Cholesterol 174 mg

Easy Chicken Salad Panini

Preparation Time: 10 minutes
Cooking Time: 5 minutes
Serve: 2

Ingredients:

- 4 bread slices
- 1 tbsp butter
- 1/4 cup pecans, toasted & chopped
- 1/2 cup apple, peel & chopped
- 3/4 cup cheddar cheese, shredded
- 1 cup cooked chicken breast, cubed
- 3/4 tsp Dijon mustard
- 3/4 tsp dill
- 1 1/2 tsp honey
- 1/4 cup mayonnaise

Directions:

1. In a small bowl, mix mayonnaise, honey, dill, and mustard.
2. In a separate bowl, mix chicken, apple, cheese, and pecans. Add mayo mixture and mix well.
3. Preheat Panini press.
4. Spread butter on one side of each bread slice.
5. Take 2 bread slices and top with chicken mixture.
6. Cover with remaining bread slices. Make sure butter side up.
7. Place sandwiches on a hot Panini press.
8. Close Panini press and cook for 5 minutes or until golden brown.
9. Serve and enjoy.

Nutritional Value (Amount per Serving):

- Calories 501
- Fat 32.9 g
- Carbohydrates 29.3 g
- Sugar 13.1 g
- Protein 23.4 g
- Cholesterol 99 mg

Healthy Turkey Panini

Preparation Time: 10 minutes
Cooking Time: 10 minutes
Serve: 4

Ingredients:

- 8 whole-wheat bread slices
- 3 cups spinach
- 1/2 onion, sliced
- 4 mozzarella cheese slices
- 4 turkey breast slices
- 1 garlic clove, minced
- 2 tbsp vinegar
- 2 tbsp olive oil

Directions:

1. In a small bowl, mix oil, garlic, and vinegar.
2. Preheat Panini press.
3. Brush one side of each bread slice with oil mixture.
4. Take 4 bread slices and top with turkey, cheese, onion, and spinach.
5. Cover with remaining bread slices. Make sure oil side up.
6. Place 2 sandwiches on a hot Panini press.
7. Close Panini press and cook for 5 minutes or until golden brown.
8. Serve and enjoy.

Nutritional Value (Amount per Serving):

- Calories 332
- Fat 14 g

- Carbohydrates 28.5 g
- Sugar 3.8 g
- Protein 23.1 g
- Cholesterol 30 mg

Avocado Turkey Cheese Panini

Preparation Time: 10 minutes
Cooking Time: 5 minutes
Serve: 1

Ingredients:

- 2 bread slices
- 1 tbsp goat cheese
- 3 oven roasted deli turkey slices
- 1/2 avocado, sliced
- 1/4 cup arugula

Directions:

1. Preheat Panini press.
2. Take 1 bread slice and top with turkey, goat cheese, avocado, and arugula.
3. Cover with remaining bread slice. Make sure butter side up.
4. Place sandwich on a hot Panini press.
5. Close Panini press and cook for 5 minutes or until golden brown.
6. Serve and enjoy.

Nutritional Value (Amount per Serving):

- Calories 479
- Fat 26.8 g
- Carbohydrates 21.2 g
- Sugar 4.6 g
- Protein 36.5 g
- Cholesterol 86 mg

Gouda Cheese Turkey Panini

Preparation Time: 10 minutes
Cooking Time: 5 minutes
Serve: 1

Ingredients:

- 2 bread slices
- 1/2 tomato slices
- 6 deli turkey meat slices
- 2 gouda cheese slices
- 1 tbsp mayonnaise
- 2 tsp butter

Directions:

1. Preheat Panini press.

2. Spread butter on one side of each bread slice.
3. Take 1 bread slice and spread with mayonnaise and top with turkey, tomato, and cheese.
4. Cover with remaining bread slice. Make sure butter side up.
5. Place sandwich on a hot Panini press.
6. Close Panini press and cook for 5 minutes or until golden brown.
7. Serve and enjoy.

Nutritional Value (Amount per Serving):

- Calories 735
- Fat 34.7 g
- Carbohydrates 32.2 g
- Sugar 21.2 g
- Protein 75.8 g
- Cholesterol 239 mg

Apple Turkey Panini

Preparation Time: 10 minutes
Cooking Time: 10 minutes
Serve: 4

Ingredients:

- 8 bread slices
- 2 tbsp butter
- 1 apple, core & thinly sliced
- 8 oz deli turkey meat slices
- 8 Swiss cheese slices
- 2 tbsp Dijon mustard

Directions:

1. Preheat Panini press.
2. Spread butter on one side of each bread slice.
3. Take 4 bread slices and spread with Dijon mustard and top with turkey, apple, and cheese.
4. Cover with remaining bread slices. Make sure buttered side up.
5. Place 2 sandwiches on a hot Panini press.
6. Close Panini press and cook for 5 minutes or until golden brown.
7. Serve and enjoy.

Nutritional Value (Amount per Serving):

- Calories 407
- Fat 23.3 g
- Carbohydrates 23.3 g
- Sugar 10.4 g
- Protein 27.1 g
- Cholesterol 92 mg

Reuben Turkey Panini

Preparation Time: 10 minutes
Cooking Time: 10 minutes
Serve: 4

Ingredients:

- 8 bread slices
- 1 cup sauerkraut, drained & squeezed
- 4 Swiss cheese slices
- 4 tsp mustard
- 6 roasted turkey breast slices
- 2 tbsp butter

Directions:

1. Preheat Panini press.
2. Spread butter on one side of each bread slice.
3. Take 4 bread slices and spread with mustard and top with turkey, sauerkraut, and cheese.
4. Cover with remaining bread slices. Make sure buttered side up.
5. Place 2 sandwiches on a hot Panini press.
6. Close Panini press and cook for 5 minutes or until golden brown.
7. Serve and enjoy.

Nutritional Value (Amount per Serving):

- Calories 317
- Fat 18.1 g
- Carbohydrates 14.8 g
- Sugar 2 g
- Protein 23.6 g
- Cholesterol 86 mg

Turkey Apricot Panini

Preparation Time: 10 minutes
Cooking Time: 10 minutes
Serve: 4

Ingredients:

- 8 bread slices
- 1 lb deli turkey slices
- 8 oz Asiago cheese
- 1 tsp sugar
- 1/2 cup balsamic vinegar
- 1 cup of water
- 2 cups dried apricots
- 2 tbsp butter

Directions:

1. In a small pot, add apricots, sugar, vinegar, and water and simmer over medium heat until the liquid reduces about 15 minutes.
2. Remove pot from heat and let it cool.
3. Once the apricot mixture is cool then transfer to a blender and blend until smooth.
4. Preheat Panini press.
5. Spread butter on one side of each bread slice.
6. Take 4 bread slices and spread with apricot mixture and top with turkey, and cheese.
7. Cover with remaining bread slices. Make sure buttered side up.
8. Place 2 sandwiches on a hot Panini press.
9. Close Panini press and cook for 5 minutes or until golden brown.
10. Serve and enjoy.

Nutritional Value (Amount per Serving):

- Calories 449
- Fat 23.1 g
- Carbohydrates 23.9 g
- Sugar 8.9 g
- Protein 34.3 g
- Cholesterol 104 mg

Chapter 5: Beef & Lamb Panini's

Beef Apple Cheese Panini

Preparation Time: 10 minutes
Cooking Time: 10 minutes
Serve: 4

Ingredients:

- 8 bread slices
- 1 apple, thinly sliced
- 6 oz cheddar cheese, sliced
- 12 oz leftover roast beef, sliced
- 2 tbsp butter
- 2 tbsp horseradish
- 3/4 cup mayonnaise

Directions:

1. In a small bowl, mix mayonnaise and horseradish.
2. Preheat Panini press.
3. Spread butter on one side of each bread slice.
4. Take 4 bread slices and spread with mayo mixture and top with beef, apple, and cheese.
5. Cover with remaining bread slices. Make sure buttered side up.
6. Place 2 sandwiches on a hot Panini press.
7. Close Panini press and cook for 5 minutes or until golden brown.
8. Serve and enjoy.

Nutritional Value (Amount per Serving):

- Calories 686
- Fat 43.7 g
- Carbohydrates 49.2 g
- Sugar 10.2 g
- Protein 25.8 g
- Cholesterol 103 mg

Easy Cheesy Beef Panini

Preparation Time: 10 minutes
Cooking Time: 5 minutes
Serve: 2

Ingredients:

- 4 bread slices
- 1/4 cup roasted bell pepper strips
- 2 tsp garlic mayonnaise
- 4 smoked Gouda cheese slices

- 6 deli roast beef slices
- 1 tbsp butter

Directions:

1. Preheat Panini press.
2. Spread butter on one side of each bread slice.
3. Take 2 bread slices and spread with mayo and top with beef, bell pepper, and cheese.
4. Cover with remaining bread slices. Make sure buttered side up.
5. Place sandwiches on a hot Panini press.
6. Close Panini press and cook for 5 minutes or until golden brown.
7. Serve and enjoy.

Nutritional Value (Amount per Serving):

- Calories 619
- Fat 24.5 g
- Carbohydrates 9.8 g
- Sugar 1.5 g
- Protein 24.8 g
- Cholesterol 92 mg

Simple Cheesesteak Panini

Preparation Time: 10 minutes
Cooking Time: 5 minutes
Serve: 1

Ingredients:

- 2 bread slices
- 2 tbsp butter
- 1/2 cup mushrooms, sliced
- 2 oz American cheese
- 6 oz shaved rib-eye steaks

Directions:

1. Melt 1 tablespoon of butter in a pan over medium heat.
2. Add mushrooms and sauté until mushroom is softened. Add sliced steaks and cook until done.
3. Preheat Panini press.
4. Spread remaining butter on one side of each bread slice.
5. Take 1 bread slice and top with mushroom and steak mixture and cheese.
6. Cover with remaining bread slice. Make sure butter side up.
7. Place sandwich on a hot Panini press.
8. Close Panini press and cook for 5 minutes or until golden brown.
9. Serve and enjoy.

Nutritional Value (Amount per Serving):

- Calories 756
- Fat 48.9 g
- Carbohydrates 14.7 g
- Sugar 5.6 g
- Protein 62.9 g
- Cholesterol 215 mg

Panera Steak Cheese Panini

Preparation Time: 10 minutes
Cooking Time: 10 minutes
Serve: 4

Ingredients:

- 8 bread slices
- 4 cheddar cheese slices
- 8 oz cooked roast beef, sliced
- 2 tbsp horseradish sauce
- 2 tbsp butter

Directions:

1. Preheat Panini press.
2. Spread butter on one side of each bread slice.
3. Take 4 bread slices and spread with horseradish sauce and top with beef and cheese.
4. Cover with remaining bread slices. Make sure buttered side up.
5. Place 2 sandwiches on a hot Panini press.
6. Close Panini press and cook for 5 minutes or until golden brown.
7. Serve and enjoy.

Nutritional Value (Amount per Serving):

- Calories 332
- Fat 20.7 g
- Carbohydrates 98 g
- Sugar 0.9 g
- Protein 25.9 g
- Cholesterol 98 mg

Meatloaf Panini

Preparation Time: 10 minutes
Cooking Time: 5 minutes
Serve: 1

Ingredients:

- 2 bread slices
- 2 cheese slices
- 1 tbsp mayonnaise
- 1 tsp butter
- 1 meatloaf slice

Directions:

1. Preheat Panini press.
2. Spread butter on one side of each bread slice.
3. Take 1 bread slice and spread with mayo top with meatloaf slice and cheese.
4. Cover with remaining bread slice. Make sure butter side up.
5. Place sandwich on a hot Panini press.
6. Close Panini press and cook for 5 minutes or until golden brown.
7. Serve and enjoy.

Nutritional Value (Amount per Serving):

- Calories 496
- Fat 30.9 g
- Carbohydrates 20.3 g
- Sugar 2 g
- Protein 33 g
- Cholesterol 73 mg

Tomato Onion Roast Beef Panini

Preparation Time: 10 minutes
Cooking Time: 10 minutes
Serve: 4

Ingredients:

- 8 bread slices
- 1 onion, sliced
- 2 tomatoes, sliced
- 8 provolone cheese slices
- 1 lb deli roast beef slices
- 1/4 cup mayonnaise
- 2 tbsp butter

Directions:

1. Preheat Panini press.
2. Spread butter on one side of each bread slice.
3. Take 4 bread slices and spread with mayo and top with beef, cheese, tomatoes, and onion.
4. Cover with remaining bread slices. Make sure buttered side up.
5. Place 2 sandwiches on a hot Panini press.
6. Close Panini press and cook for 5 minutes or until golden brown.
7. Serve and enjoy.

Nutritional Value (Amount per Serving):

- Calories 375
- Fat 32.3 g
- Carbohydrates 18.8 g
- Sugar 4.8 g

- Protein 54.5 g
- Cholesterol 157 mg

Leftover Roast Beef Panini

Preparation Time: 10 minutes
Cooking Time: 10 minutes
Serve: 4

Ingredients:

- 8 bread slices
- 1/4 cup onion, sliced
- 2 cheese slices, cut in half
- 1 cup baby arugula
- 8 oz leftover cooked roast beef, sliced
- 2 tbsp mayonnaise
- 1/8 tsp caraway seeds
- 1 tsp Dijon mustard
- 1 tbsp prepared horseradish
- 2 tbsp butter

Directions:

1. In a small bowl, mix together mayonnaise, caraway seeds, mustard, and horseradish.
2. Preheat Panini press.
3. Spread butter on one side of each bread slice.
4. Take 4 bread slices and spread with mayo and top with beef, arugula, cheese, and onion.
5. Cover with remaining bread slices. Make sure buttered side up.
6. Place 2 sandwiches on a hot Panini press.
7. Close Panini press and cook for 5 minutes or until golden brown.
8. Serve and enjoy.

Nutritional Value (Amount per Serving):

- Calories 262
- Fat 15.1 g
- Carbohydrates 13.4 g
- Sugar 3 g
- Protein 15.4 g
- Cholesterol 57 mg

Spinach Roast Beef Panini

Preparation Time: 10 minutes
Cooking Time: 5 minutes
Serve: 1

Ingredients:

- 2 bread slices
- 2 tomato slices
- 1/4 tsp horseradish
- 1 tsp mayonnaise

- 1 cheddar cheese slice
- 2 oz roast beef
- 1/4 cup baby spinach
- 2 tsp butter

Directions:

1. In a small bowl, mix together mayonnaise and horseradish.
2. Preheat Panini press.
3. Spread butter on one side of each bread slice.
4. Take 1 bread slice and spread with mayo mixture top with beef, tomato, spinach, and cheese.
5. Cover with remaining bread slice. Make sure butter side up.
6. Place sandwich on a hot Panini press.
7. Close Panini press and cook for 5 minutes or until golden brown.
8. Serve and enjoy.

Nutritional Value (Amount per Serving):

- Calories 360
- Fat 22.8 g
- Carbohydrates 12.2 g
- Sugar 2.2 g
- Protein 26.2 g
- Cholesterol 102 mg

Gouda Cheese Roast Beef Panini

Preparation Time: 10 minutes
Cooking Time: 10 minutes
Serve: 4

Ingredients:

- 8 bread slices
- 1 cup watercress sprigs
- 1/2 lb deli roast beef, sliced
- 2 oz smoked gouda cheese, shredded
- 2 tsp Dijon mustard
- 8 tbsp hot pepper jelly
- 2 tbsp butter

Directions:

1. Preheat Panini press.
2. Spread butter on one side of each bread slice.
3. Take 4 bread slices and spread with mustard and jelly and top with beef, watercress, and cheese.
4. Cover with remaining bread slices. Make sure buttered side up.
5. Place 2 sandwiches on a hot Panini press.
6. Close Panini press and cook for 5 minutes or until golden brown.
7. Serve and enjoy.

Nutritional Value (Amount per Serving):

- Calories 326
- Fat 13.9 g
- Carbohydrates 27.6 g
- Sugar 17.1 g
- Protein 22.3 g
- Cholesterol 82 mg

Delicious Apple Beef Panini

Preparation Time: 10 minutes
Cooking Time: 5 minutes
Serve: 2

Ingredients:

- 4 bread slices
- 4 oz deli roast beef, sliced
- 1/2 apple, sliced
- 2 tsp horseradish sauce
- 2 cheddar cheese slices
- 1 tbsp butter

Directions:

1. Preheat Panini press.
2. Spread butter on one side of each bread slice.
3. Take 2 bread slices and spread with horseradish sauce and top with cheese, beef, and apple.
4. Cover with remaining bread slices. Make sure buttered side up.
5. Place sandwiches on a hot Panini press.
6. Close Panini press and cook for 5 minutes or until golden brown.
7. Serve and enjoy.

Nutritional Value (Amount per Serving):

- Calories 376
- Fat 22.3 g
- Carbohydrates 18.2 g
- Sugar 6.7 g
- Protein 25.8 g
- Cholesterol 100 mg

Leftover Lamb Panini

Preparation Time: 10 minutes
Cooking Time: 5 minutes
Serve: 1

Ingredients:

- 2 bread slices
- 2 tbsp tzatziki

- 1/4 cup spinach
- 2 onion sliced
- 1/4 cup leftover lamb, reheated
- 1/2 cup Havarti cheese, shredded
- 1 tbsp butter

Directions:

1. Preheat Panini press.
2. Spread butter on one side of each bread slice.
3. Take 1 bread slice and spread with tzatziki top with lamb, onion, spinach, and cheese.
4. Cover with remaining bread slice. Make sure butter side up.
5. Place sandwich on a hot Panini press.
6. Close Panini press and cook for 5 minutes or until golden brown.
7. Serve and enjoy.

Nutritional Value (Amount per Serving):

- Calories 302
- Fat 22.7 g
- Carbohydrates 13.6 g
- Sugar 3.1 g
- Protein 12.1 g
- Cholesterol 69 mg

Caramelized Onion Cheese Steak Panini

Preparation Time: 10 minutes
Cooking Time: 5 minutes
Serve: 2

Ingredients:

- 4 bread slices
- 1 tbsp butter
- 2 tbsp mayonnaise
- 2 tbsp caramelized onion
- 3 oz Fontina cheese, sliced
- 8 oz steak, cooked & sliced

Directions:

1. Preheat Panini press.
2. Spread butter on one side of each bread slice.
3. Take 2 bread slices and spread with mayo and top with steak, onion, and cheese.
4. Cover with remaining bread slices. Make sure buttered side up.
5. Place sandwiches on a hot Panini press.
6. Close Panini press and cook for 5 minutes or until golden brown.
7. Serve and enjoy.

Nutritional Value (Amount per Serving):

- Calories 556
- Fat 30.4 g
- Carbohydrates 14.8 g
- Sugar 3.3 g
- Protein 53.7 g
- Cholesterol 170 mg

Slaw Roast Beef Panini

Preparation Time: 10 minutes
Cooking Time: 10 minutes
Serve: 4

Ingredients:

- 8 bread slices
- 2 tbsp butter
- 1/2 lb deli roast beef, sliced
- 1/4 tsp caraway seeds
- 1/2 tbsp mustard
- 1 tbsp horseradish
- 3 tbsp mayonnaise
- 1 1/2 cups coleslaw
- 4 cheddar cheese slices
- 1/4 cup sun-dried tomatoes, drained & cut into strips

Directions:

1. Preheat Panini press.
2. Spread butter on one side of each bread slice.
3. In a bowl, mix coleslaw, caraway seeds, mustard, horseradish, mayonnaise, and sun-dried tomatoes.
4. Take 4 bread slices and top with beef, cheese, and coleslaw mixture.
5. Cover with remaining bread slices. Make sure buttered side up.
6. Place 2 sandwiches on a hot Panini press.
7. Close Panini press and cook for 5 minutes or until golden brown.
8. Serve and enjoy.

Nutritional Value (Amount per Serving):

- Calories 444
- Fat 28.8 g
- Carbohydrates 19.9 g
- Sugar 2.3 g
- Protein 27 g
- Cholesterol 101 mg

Chipotle Roast Beef Panini

Preparation Time: 10 minutes
Cooking Time: 5 minutes
Serve: 1

Ingredients:

- 2 bread slices
- 1 tbsp chipotle mayonnaise
- 1/4 cup caramelized onions, sliced
- 2 gouda cheese slices
- 4 deli roast beef, sliced
- 2 tsp butter

Directions:

1. Preheat Panini press.
2. Spread butter on one side of each bread slice.
3. Take 1 bread slice and spread with mayo top with beef, onion, and cheese.
4. Cover with remaining bread slice. Make sure butter side up.
5. Place sandwich on a hot Panini press.
6. Close Panini press and cook for 5 minutes or until golden brown.
7. Serve and enjoy.

Nutritional Value (Amount per Serving):

- Calories 446
- Fat 41.7 g
- Carbohydrates 10.6 g
- Sugar 2.2 g
- Protein 6.5 g
- Cholesterol 63 mg

Chimichurri Steak Panini

Preparation Time: 10 minutes
Cooking Time: 10 minutes
Serve: 4

Ingredients:

- 1/2 lb steaks, cooked & sliced
- 8 bread slices
- 8 provolone cheese slices
- 4 tbsp chimichurri sauce
- 2 tbsp butter

Directions:

1. Preheat Panini press.
2. Spread butter on one side of each bread slice.
3. Take 4 bread slices and spread with chimichurri sauce and top with steak and cheese.
4. Cover with remaining bread slices. Make sure buttered side up.
5. Place 2 sandwiches on a hot Panini press.
6. Close Panini press and cook for 5 minutes or until golden brown.
7. Serve and enjoy.

Nutritional Value (Amount per Serving):

- Calories 408
- Fat 24.1 g
- Carbohydrates 10.3 g
- Sugar 1.1 g
- Protein 36.2 g
- Cholesterol 105 mg

Horseradish Roast Beef Panini

Preparation Time: 10 minutes
Cooking Time: 15 minutes
Serve: 6

Ingredients:

- 12 bread slices
- 3 oz cheddar cheese slices
- 9 oz sliced roast beef
- 3 tbsp chives, minced
- 1/2 cup crème Fraiche
- 3 tbsp horseradish cream
- 3 tbsp butter
- 1/4 tsp salt

Directions:

1. In a bowl, mix crème Fraiche, horseradish cream, chives, and salt.
2. Preheat Panini press.
3. Spread butter on one side of each bread slice.
4. Take 6 bread slices and spread with crème Fraiche mixture and top with beef and cheese.
5. Cover with remaining bread slices. Make sure buttered side up.
6. Place 2 sandwiches on a hot Panini press.
7. Close Panini press and cook for 5 minutes or until golden brown.
8. Serve and enjoy.

Nutritional Value (Amount per Serving):

- Calories 276
- Fat 17.7 g
- Carbohydrates 10.9 g
- Sugar 1.4 g
- Protein 18.4 g
- Cholesterol 75 mg

Tasty Reuben Panini

Preparation Time: 10 minutes
Cooking Time: 10 minutes
Serve: 4

Ingredients:

- 8 bread slices
- 6 oz Gruyere cheese, shredded
- 10 oz sauerkraut
- 1 lb cooked corned beef, sliced
- 2 tbsp butter
- 1/2 tsp sriracha sauce
- 1 tbsp sweet pickle relish
- 1 tbsp ketchup
- 3 tbsp mayonnaise

Directions:

1. In a small bowl, mix mayonnaise, sriracha, pickle relish, and ketchup.
2. Preheat Panini press.
3. Spread butter on one side of each bread slice.
4. Take 4 bread slices and spread with mayo and top with beef, sauerkraut, and cheese.
5. Cover with remaining bread slices. Make sure buttered side up.
6. Place 2 sandwiches on a hot Panini press.
7. Close Panini press and cook for 5 minutes or until golden brown.
8. Serve and enjoy.

Nutritional Value (Amount per Serving):

- Calories 532
- Fat 38.1 g
- Carbohydrates 17.2 g
- Sugar 4.8 g
- Protein 30.1 g
- Cholesterol 136 mg

Gorgonzola Mayo Roast Beef Panini

Preparation Time: 10 minutes
Cooking Time: 10 minutes
Serve: 4

Ingredients:

- 8 bread slices
- 2 tbsp butter
- 8 fontina cheese slices
- 12 oz sweet roasted red peppers
- 4 oz baby spinach
- 1/4 cup gorgonzola cheese, crumbled
- 1 garlic clove, chopped
- 1/2 cup mayonnaise
- 3/4 lb deli roast beef, sliced

Directions:

1. In a small bowl, mix mayonnaise, gorgonzola cheese, and garlic.
2. Preheat Panini press.
3. Spread butter on one side of each bread slice.
4. Take 4 bread slices and spread with mayo and top with beef, spinach, roasted peppers, and cheese.

5. Cover with remaining bread slices. Make sure buttered side up.
6. Place 2 sandwiches on a hot Panini press.
7. Close Panini press and cook for 5 minutes or until golden brown.
8. Serve and enjoy.

Nutritional Value (Amount per Serving):

- Calories 659
- Fat 42 g
- Carbohydrates 24.1 g
- Sugar 8.8 g
- Protein 46.1 g
- Cholesterol 174 mg

Easy Classic Reuben Panini

Preparation Time: 10 minutes
Cooking Time: 10 minutes
Serve: 4

Ingredients:

- 8 bread slices
- 8 Swiss cheese slices
- 1/2 lb corned beef, sliced
- 1 cup sauerkraut, drained & squeezed
- 1/4 cup Island dressing
- 2 tbsp butter

Directions:

1. Preheat Panini press.
2. Spread butter on one side of each bread slice.
3. Take 4 bread slices and spread with dressing and top with beef, sauerkraut, and cheese.
4. Cover with remaining bread slices. Make sure buttered side up.
5. Place 2 sandwiches on a hot Panini press.
6. Close Panini press and cook for 5 minutes or until golden brown.
7. Serve and enjoy.

Nutritional Value (Amount per Serving):

- Calories 455
- Fat 33.1 g
- Carbohydrates 14.1 g
- Sugar 2.2 g
- Protein 24.4 g
- Cholesterol 217 mg

Southwestern Roast Beef Panini

Preparation Time: 10 minutes
Cooking Time: 5 minutes

Serve: 2

Ingredients:

- 4 bread slices
- 2 tbsp can whole green chilies, halved
- 2 pepper jack cheese slices
- 4 oz cooked roast beef slices
- 1 tbsp butter

Directions:

1. Preheat Panini press.
2. Spread butter on one side of each bread slice.
3. Take 2 bread slices and top with beef, cheese, and chilies.
4. Cover with remaining bread slices. Make sure buttered side up.
5. Place sandwiches on a hot Panini press.
6. Close Panini press and cook for 5 minutes or until golden brown.
7. Serve and enjoy.

Nutritional Value (Amount per Serving):

- Calories 559
- Fat 32.5 g
- Carbohydrates 16.5 g
- Sugar 4.9 g
- Protein 50.9 g
- Cholesterol 45 mg

Chapter 6: Pork Panini's

Easy Pork Panini

Preparation Time: 10 minutes
Cooking Time: 10 minutes
Serve: 4

Ingredients:

- 8 bread slices
- 2 tbsp butter
- 4 oz provolone cheese slices
- 1/2 cup pesto
- 3 pork chops, cooked & sliced

Directions:

1. Preheat Panini press.
2. Spread butter on one side of each bread slice.
3. Take 4 bread slices and spread with pesto and top with pork and cheese.
4. Cover with remaining bread slices. Make sure buttered side up.
5. Place 2 sandwiches on a hot Panini press.
6. Close Panini press and cook for 5 minutes or until golden brown.
7. Serve and enjoy.

Nutritional Value (Amount per Serving):

- Calories 527
- Fat 42.4 g
- Carbohydrates 12.1 g
- Sugar 2.8 g
- Protein 25 g
- Cholesterol 100 mg

Cuban Panini

Preparation Time: 10 minutes
Cooking Time: 5 minutes
Serve: 1

Ingredients:

- 2 bread slices
- 1 tbsp butter
- 1 roasted pork slice
- 2 ham slices
- 1 fontina cheese slice
- 1 Swiss cheese slice
- 2 tbsp sweet banana peppers, sliced
- 2 tbsp jalapeno peppers, sliced
- 2 tbsp honey mustard

Directions:

1. Preheat Panini press.
2. Spread butter on one side of each bread slice.
3. Take 1 bread slice and spread with honey mustard top with pork slice, jalapeno peppers, sweet banana peppers, ham, and cheese.
4. Cover with remaining bread slice. Make sure butter side up.
5. Place sandwich on a hot Panini press.
6. Close Panini press and cook for 5 minutes or until golden brown.
7. Serve and enjoy.

Nutritional Value (Amount per Serving):

- Calories 740
- Fat 47.6 g
- Carbohydrates 27.8 g
- Sugar 7.9 g
- Protein 45.6 g
- Cholesterol 191 mg

Prosciutto Egg Panini

Preparation Time: 10 minutes
Cooking Time: 10 minutes
Serve: 4

Ingredients:

- 4 eggs
- 8 bread slices
- 3 tbsp butter
- 1/4 cup raspberry jam
- 16 prosciutto slices
- 8 oz provolone cheese, sliced

Directions:

1. In a shallow dish, whisk eggs.
2. Preheat Panini press.
3. Spread butter on one side of each bread slice.
4. Take 4 bread slices and spread with raspberry jam and top with prosciutto and cheese.
5. Cover with remaining bread slices. Make sure buttered side up.
6. Dip 2 sandwiches in egg and place on a hot Panini press.
7. Close Panini press and cook for 5 minutes or until golden brown.
8. Serve and enjoy.

Nutritional Value (Amount per Serving):

- Calories 361
- Fat 17.5 g

- Carbohydrates 25.3 g
- Sugar 10.3 g
- Protein 25.4 g
- Cholesterol 218 mg

Cheddar Apple Pork Panini

Preparation Time: 10 minutes
Cooking Time: 10 minutes
Serve: 4

Ingredients:

- 8 pork chops, boneless, cooked & sliced
- 4 oz cheddar cheese, sliced
- 1 apple, core & slice
- 3 tbsp butter
- 8 bread slices
- 2 tbsp Dijon mustard
- 4 tbsp apricot preserves

Directions:

1. Preheat Panini press.
2. Spread butter on one side of each bread slice.
3. Take 4 bread slices and spread with Dijon mustard and apricot preserves and top with pork, apple, and cheese.
4. Cover with remaining bread slices. Make sure buttered side up.
5. Place 2 sandwiches on a hot Panini press.
6. Close Panini press and cook for 5 minutes or until golden brown.
7. Serve and enjoy.

Nutritional Value (Amount per Serving):

- Calories 833
- Fat 58.8 g
- Carbohydrates 30.5 g
- Sugar 15.5 g
- Protein 45.1 g
- Cholesterol 190 mg

Apple Ham Panini

Preparation Time: 10 minutes
Cooking Time: 5 minutes
Serve: 2

Ingredients:

- 4 bread slices
- 2 gouda cheese slices
- 1/2 apple, sliced
- 6 deli smoked ham slices
- 1 tbsp butter

Directions:

1. Preheat Panini press.
2. Spread butter on one side of each bread slice.
3. Take 2 bread slices and top with ham, apple, and cheese.
4. Cover with remaining bread slices. Make sure buttered side up.
5. Place sandwiches on a hot Panini press.
6. Close Panini press and cook for 5 minutes or until golden brown.
7. Serve and enjoy.

Nutritional Value (Amount per Serving):

- Calories 310
- Fat 12.6 g
- Carbohydrates 19.8 g
- Sugar 9.6 g
- Protein 28.7 g
- Cholesterol 91 mg

Apple Ham Gruyere Panini

Preparation Time: 10 minutes
Cooking Time: 10 minutes
Serve: 4

Ingredients:

- 8 bread slices
- 8 ham slices
- 2 cups Gruyere cheese, shredded
- 1/2 cup Dijon mustard
- 1 tbsp thyme, chopped
- 2 apples, peel, core, & sliced
- 4 tbsp butter

Directions:

1. Melt 2 tablespoons of butter in a pan over medium heat.
2. Add apples and thyme and cook for 4 minutes.
3. Preheat Panini press.
4. Spread butter on one side of each bread slice.
5. Take 4 bread slices and spread with Dijon mustard and top with ham, apples, and cheese.
6. Cover with remaining bread slices. Make sure buttered side up.
7. Place 2 sandwiches on a hot Panini press.
8. Close Panini press and cook for 5 minutes or until golden brown.
9. Serve and enjoy.

Nutritional Value (Amount per Serving):

- Calories 545
- Fat 35.9 g
- Carbohydrates 29 g
- Sugar 12.9 g
- Protein 28.6 g
- Cholesterol 122 mg

Delicious Ham Serrano Panini

Preparation Time: 10 minutes
Cooking Time: 5 minutes
Serve: 1

Ingredients:

- 2 bread slices
- 1 tbsp butter
- 1 tsp Dijon mustard
- 2 Serrano ham slices
- 2 provolone cheese slices

Directions:

1. Preheat Panini press.
2. Spread butter on one side of each bread slice.
3. Take 1 bread slice and spread with mustard and top with ham and cheese.
4. Cover with remaining bread slice. Make sure butter side up.
5. Place sandwich on a hot Panini press.
6. Close Panini press and cook for 5 minutes or until golden brown.
7. Serve and enjoy.

Nutritional Value (Amount per Serving):

- Calories 441
- Fat 32 g
- Carbohydrates 12.7 g
- Sugar 1.1 g
- Protein 25.3 g
- Cholesterol 101 mg

Pesto Prosciutto Panini

Preparation Time: 10 minutes
Cooking Time: 5 minutes
Serve: 2

Ingredients:

- 4 bread slices
- 1/4 lb provolone cheese, sliced
- 1/4 lb prosciutto, sliced
- 1 cup baby spinach
- 2 tbsp pesto
- 2 tbsp mayonnaise
- 1 tbsp butter

Directions:

1. Preheat Panini press.
2. In a small bowl, mayonnaise, and pesto.
3. Spread butter on one side of each bread slice.
4. Take 2 bread slices and spread with mayo and top with prosciutto, spinach, and cheese.
5. Cover with remaining bread slices. Make sure buttered side up.
6. Place sandwiches on a hot Panini press.
7. Close Panini press and cook for 5 minutes or until golden brown.
8. Serve and enjoy.

Nutritional Value (Amount per Serving):

- Calories 508
- Fat 36.1 g
- Carbohydrates 16.2 g
- Sugar 3.1 g
- Protein 29.9 g
- Cholesterol 92 mg

Ham Jalapeno Popper Panini

Preparation Time: 10 minutes
Cooking Time: 5 minutes
Serve: 1

Ingredients:

- 2 bread slices
- 2 roasted jalapenos
- 1 pepper jack cheese slice
- 2 tbsp cream cheese
- 4 deli ham slices
- 2 tsp butter

Directions:

1. Preheat Panini press.
2. Spread butter on one side of each bread slice.
3. Take 1 bread slice and spread with cream cheese and top with ham, jalapenos, and cheese.
4. Cover with remaining bread slice. Make sure butter side up.
5. Place sandwich on a hot Panini press.
6. Close Panini press and cook for 5 minutes or until golden brown.
7. Serve and enjoy.

Nutritional Value (Amount per Serving):

- Calories 478
- Fat 33.8 g

- Carbohydrates 13.9 g
- Sugar 0.8 g
- Protein 28.6 g
- Cholesterol 136 mg

Pear Prosciutto Panini

Preparation Time: 10 minutes
Cooking Time: 5 minutes
Serve: 2

Ingredients:

- 4 bread slices
- 1 tbsp butter
- 4 oz goat cheese, crumbled
- 1 ripe pear, sliced
- 3 oz Prosciutto

Directions:

1. Preheat Panini press.
2. Spread butter on one side of each bread slice.
3. Take 2 bread slices and top with prosciutto, pear, and cheese.
4. Cover with remaining bread slices. Make sure buttered side up.
5. Place sandwiches on a hot Panini press.
6. Close Panini press and cook for 5 minutes or until golden brown.
7. Serve and enjoy.

Nutritional Value (Amount per Serving):

- Calories 457
- Fat 29 g
- Carbohydrates 21.6 g
- Sugar 8.8 g
- Protein 27.9 g
- Cholesterol 97 mg

Pear Ham Panini

Preparation Time: 10 minutes
Cooking Time: 5 minutes
Serve: 1

Ingredients:

- 2 bread slices
- 1/2 tbsp maple syrup
- 1/2 tbsp Dijon mustard
- 2 tbsp mayonnaise
- 1/2 pear, sliced
- 2 Swiss cheese slices
- 5 deli ham slices
- 2 tsp butter

Directions:

1. In a small bowl, mayonnaise, Dijon mustard, and maple syrup.
2. Preheat Panini press.
3. Spread butter on one side of each bread slice.
4. Take 1 bread slice and spread with mayo and top with ham, pear, and cheese.
5. Cover with remaining bread slice. Make sure butter side up.
6. Place sandwich on a hot Panini press.
7. Close Panini press and cook for 5 minutes or until golden brown.
8. Serve and enjoy.

Nutritional Value (Amount per Serving):

- Calories 441
- Fat 27.5 g
- Carbohydrates 34.9 g
- Sugar 16.5 g
- Protein 17.3 g
- Cholesterol 73 mg

Provolone Prosciutto Panini

Preparation Time: 10 minutes
Cooking Time: 10 minutes
Serve: 4

Ingredients:

- 8 bread slices
- 8 oz prosciutto slices
- 12 provolone cheese slices
- 2 tbsp butter
- 2 tsp rosemary, chopped
- 2 red bell peppers, cut into strips

Directions:

1. Preheat Panini press.
2. Spread butter on one side of each bread slice.
3. Take 4 bread slices and top with prosciutto, rosemary, bell peppers, and cheese.
4. Cover with remaining bread slices. Make sure buttered side up.
5. Place 2 sandwiches on a hot Panini press.
6. Close Panini press and cook for 5 minutes or until golden brown.
7. Serve and enjoy.

Nutritional Value (Amount per Serving):

- Calories 536
- Fat 36 g
- Carbohydrates 15.8 g
- Sugar 4.3 g
- Protein 38.8 g
- Cholesterol 124 mg

Pulled Pork Panini

Preparation Time: 10 minutes
Cooking Time: 15 minutes
Serve: 6

Ingredients:

- 12 bread slices
- 4 tbsp butter
- 8 oz Colby Jack cheese, shredded
- 1 lb cooked pork, shredded
- 1/2 cup hot sauce

Directions:

1. Preheat Panini press.
2. Spread butter on one side of each bread slice.
3. Take 6 bread slices and spread with hot sauce and top with pork and cheese.
4. Cover with remaining bread slices. Make sure buttered side up.
5. Place 2 sandwiches on a hot Panini press.
6. Close Panini press and cook for 5 minutes or until golden brown.
7. Serve and enjoy.

Nutritional Value (Amount per Serving):

- Calories 373
- Fat 23 g
- Carbohydrates 10.8 g
- Sugar 1 g
- Protein 29.4 g
- Cholesterol 109 mg

Cuban Style Cheese Panini

Preparation Time: 10 minutes
Cooking Time: 5 minutes
Serve: 2

Ingredients:

- 4 bread slices
- 2 tbsp dill pickles, chopped
- 2 oz cooked pork slices
- 1 oz deli ham slice
- 3 oz cheddar cheese, sliced
- 1 tbsp mayonnaise
- 1 tbsp Dijon mustard
- 1 tbsp butter

Directions:

1. In a small bowl, mix together mayonnaise and Dijon mustard.

2. Preheat Panini press.
3. Spread butter on one side of each bread slice.
4. Take 2 bread slices and spread with mayo and top with ham, pork, dill pickles, and cheese.
5. Cover with remaining bread slices. Make sure buttered side up.
6. Place sandwiches on a hot Panini press.
7. Close Panini press and cook for 5 minutes or until golden brown.
8. Serve and enjoy.

Nutritional Value (Amount per Serving):

- Calories 521
- Fat 38.2 g
- Carbohydrates 14.5 g
- Sugar 3.4 g
- Protein 30.1 g
- Cholesterol 68 mg

Greek Pork Panini

Preparation Time: 10 minutes
Cooking Time: 5 minutes
Serve: 2

Ingredients:

- 4 bread slices
- 2 oz cheddar cheese, sliced
- 2 tbsp olive tapenade
- 6 oz porchetta
- 1 tbsp butter

Directions:

1. Preheat Panini press.
2. Spread butter on one side of each bread slice.
3. Take 2 bread slices and top with olive tapenade, porchetta, and cheese.
4. Cover with remaining bread slices. Make sure buttered side up.
5. Place sandwiches on a hot Panini press.
6. Close Panini press and cook for 5 minutes or until golden brown.
7. Serve and enjoy.

Nutritional Value (Amount per Serving):

- Calories 675
- Fat 57.9 g
- Carbohydrates 12.5 g
- Sugar 2.4 g
- Protein 23.4 g
- Cholesterol 98 mg

Chapter 7: Bruschetta Panini's

Garlic Bread Bruschetta

Preparation Time: 10 minutes
Cooking Time: 10 minutes
Serve: 8

Ingredients:

- 8 Italian bread slices
- 1 garlic clove, minced
- 1/4 cup olive oil
- For salad:
- 1 tbsp balsamic vinegar
- 1 tbsp olive oil
- 2 garlic cloves, minced
- 1/4 cup basil, sliced
- 1/4 cup parmesan cheese, grated
- 2 cups cherry tomatoes, diced
- Pepper
- Salt

Directions:

1. Preheat Panini press.
2. In a small bowl, mix olive oil and garlic.
3. Brush bread slices with oil and place on a hot Panini press. In batches.
4. Close Panini press and cook for 8-10 minutes or until golden brown.
5. In a mixing bowl, mix all salad ingredients.
6. Divide salad over toasted bread slices and serve.

Nutritional Value (Amount per Serving):

- Calories 118
- Fat 9 g
- Carbohydrates 8 g
- Sugar 1.6 g
- Protein 2.4 g
- Cholesterol 2 mg

Tomato Bruschetta

Preparation Time: 10 minutes
Cooking Time: 10 minutes
Serve: 4

Ingredients:

- 8 oz baguette bread, cut into 1-inch slices
- 2 tbsp olive oil
- 2 tbsp garlic, minced

For topping:

- 4 oz mozzarella cheese, shredded
- 0.5 oz basil, chopped
- 2 oz onions, chopped
- 8 oz tomato, chopped
- 2 tsp honey
- 4 tbsp balsamic vinegar
- 1/8 tsp salt

Directions:

1. Preheat Panini press.
2. In a small bowl, mix olive oil and garlic.
3. Brush bread slices with oil and place on a hot Panini press. In batches.
4. Close Panini press and cook for 8-10 minutes or until golden brown.
5. In a mixing bowl, mix all topping ingredients.
6. Divide topping mixture over toasted bread slices and serve.

Nutritional Value (Amount per Serving):

- Calories 327
- Fat 12.2 g
- Carbohydrates 38 g
- Sugar 6.2 g
- Protein 14.8 g
- Cholesterol 15 mg

Mushroom Bruschetta

Preparation Time: 10 minutes
Cooking Time: 10 minutes
Serve: 12

Ingredients:

- 1 sourdough baguette, cut into 1/2-inch slices
- 2 tbsp olive oil
- For spread:
- 2 tbsp heavy cream
- 5 oz goat cheese, 1 lemon zest
- For topping:
- 2 cups mushrooms, sliced
- 1/2 stick butter
- Pepper
- Salt

Directions:

1. Preheat Panini press.
2. Brush bread slices with oil and place on a hot Panini press. In batches.
3. Close Panini press and cook for 8-10 minutes or until golden brown.
4. For the spread: add cream and goat cheese in a blender and blend until smooth.
5. For mushrooms: Melt butter in a pan over medium heat.
6. Add mushrooms to the pan and sauté until golden brown. Season with pepper and salt.

7. Spread cheese mixture over toasted bread slices and top with mushrooms.
8. Serve and enjoy.

Nutritional Value (Amount per Serving):

- Calories 134
- Fat 11.4 g
- Carbohydrates 3.7 g
- Sugar 0.6 g
- Protein 4.7 g
- Cholesterol 26 mg

Artichoke Spinach Bruschetta

Preparation Time: 10 minutes
Cooking Time: 10 minutes
Serve: 4

Ingredients:

- 8 oz baguette bread, cut into 1-inch slices
- 2 tbsp olive oil
- For topping:
- 1/4 cup mayonnaise
- 4 garlic cloves, chopped
- 1/4 cup Asiago cheese, grated
- 1 cup can artichokes, drained & chopped
- 2 cups spinach, chopped
- 1/2 tsp salt

Directions:

1. Preheat Panini press.
2. Brush bread slices with oil and place on a hot Panini press. In batches.
3. Close Panini press and cook for 8-10 minutes or until golden brown.
4. In a mixing bowl, add all topping ingredients and mix well.
5. Spoon topping mixture over toasted bread slices and cook for 5 minutes more.
6. Serve and enjoy.

Nutritional Value (Amount per Serving):

- Calories 297
- Fat 12.6 g
- Carbohydrates 35.7 g
- Sugar 2.5 g
- Protein 7.8 g
- Cholesterol 5 mg

Artichoke Bruschetta

Preparation Time: 10 minutes
Cooking Time: 10 minutes
Serve: 4

Ingredients:

- 8 oz baguette bread, cut into 1-inch slices
- 2 tbsp olive oil
- For topping:
- 1/2 cup mozzarella cheese, grated
- 1/2 cup parmesan cheese, grated
- 7 oz can artichoke hearts, drained & chopped
- 1/2 cup mayonnaise
- 4 oz cream cheese
- 1/2 tsp garlic salt

Directions:

1. Preheat Panini press.
2. Brush bread slices with oil and place on a hot Panini press. In batches.
3. Close Panini press and cook for 8-10 minutes or until golden brown.
4. In a bowl, add cream cheese and beat until smooth. Add mozzarella cheese, parmesan cheese, artichoke hearts, mayonnaise, and salt and mix well.
5. Spoon topping mixture over toasted bread slices and cook for 2-3 minutes more.
6. Serve and enjoy.

Nutritional Value (Amount per Serving):

- Calories 486
- Fat 29.7 g
- Carbohydrates 40 g
- Sugar 3.6 g
- Protein 13.7 g
- Cholesterol 49 mg

Mango Pineapple Bruschetta

Preparation Time: 10 minutes
Cooking Time: 10 minutes
Serve: 4

Ingredients:

- 8 oz baguette bread, cut into 1-inch slices
- 2 tbsp olive oil
- For topping:
- 1 cup can pineapple, chopped
- 1/2 lime juice
- 2 tbsp cilantro, chopped
- 1/4 onion, diced
- 1/2 bell pepper, diced
- 1 mango, peel & dice
- Salt

Directions:

1. Preheat Panini press.
2. Brush bread slices with oil and place on a hot Panini press. In batches.

3. Close Panini press and cook for 8-10 minutes or until golden brown.
4. In a bowl, add all topping ingredients and mix well.
5. Spoon topping mixture over toasted bread slices and serve.

Nutritional Value (Amount per Serving):

- Calories 307
- Fat 7.4 g
- Carbohydrates 53.5 g
- Sugar 22.8 g
- Protein 7 g
- Cholesterol 0 mg

Cannellini Bean Bruschetta

Preparation Time: 10 minutes
Cooking Time: 10 minutes
Serve: 4

Ingredients:

- 4 sourdough bread slices
- 1 tbsp olive oil
- For topping:
- 14 oz can cannellini beans, drained & mashed
- 1 tbsp parsley, chopped
- 1 1/2 tbsp lemon juice
- 1/2 lemon zest
- Pepper
- Salt

Directions:

1. Preheat Panini press.
2. Brush bread slices with oil and place on a hot Panini press. In batches.
3. Close Panini press and cook for 8-10 minutes or until golden brown.
4. In a bowl, add all topping ingredients and mix well.
5. Spoon topping mixture over toasted bread slices and serve.

Nutritional Value (Amount per Serving):

- Calories 199
- Fat 4.9 g
- Carbohydrates 31.1 g
- Sugar 1.1 g
- Protein 8.3 g
- Cholesterol 0 mg

Avocado Bruschetta

Preparation Time: 10 minutes
Cooking Time: 10 minutes
Serve: 6

Ingredients:

- 6 sourdough bread slices
- 2 tbsp olive oil
- For topping:
- 1 cucumber, diced
- 1/4 cup basil, chopped
- 1 tbsp balsamic vinegar
- 1 avocado, peel & dice
- 1 tomato, chopped
- 1 garlic clove, minced
- 1/4 tsp sea salt

Directions:

1. Preheat Panini press.
2. Brush bread slices with oil and place on a hot Panini press. In batches.
3. Close Panini press and cook for 8-10 minutes or until golden brown.
4. In a bowl, add all topping ingredients and mix well.
5. Spoon topping mixture over toasted bread slices and serve.

Nutritional Value (Amount per Serving):

- Calories 212
- Fat 11.9 g
- Carbohydrates 23.4 g
- Sugar 2.1 g
- Protein 4.9 g
- Cholesterol 0 mg

Strawberry Cheese Bruschetta

Preparation Time: 10 minutes
Cooking Time: 10 minutes
Serve: 8

Ingredients:

- 8 oz baguette bread, cut into 1-inch slices
- 2 tbsp olive oil
- For topping:
- 2 tbsp balsamic glaze
- 1 tbsp basil, chopped
- 1/2 cup goat cheese, crumbled
- 1/2 cup strawberries, sliced
- Pepper
- Salt

Directions:

1. Brush bread slices with oil and place on a hot Panini press. In batches.
2. Close Panini press and cook for 8-10 minutes or until golden brown.
3. In a bowl, add all topping ingredients and mix well.
4. Spoon topping mixture over toasted bread slices and serve.

Nutritional Value (Amount per Serving):

- Calories 117
- Fat 4.2 g
- Carbohydrates 16.2 g
- Sugar 1.8 g
- Protein 3.5 g
- Cholesterol 2 mg

Lemon Avocado Bruschetta

Preparation Time: 10 minutes
Cooking Time: 10 minutes
Serve: 8

Ingredients:

- 8 French bread slices
- 2 tbsp olive oil
- For topping:
- 8 Roma tomatoes, diced
- 1 tsp olive oil
- 1 tbsp balsamic vinegar
- 2 garlic cloves, minced
- 1/3 cup basil, chopped
- 1/2 tsp lemon juice
- 3 avocados, diced
- 1/4 tsp salt

Directions:

1. Preheat Panini press.
2. Brush bread slices with oil and place on a hot Panini press. In batches.
3. Close Panini press and cook for 8-10 minutes or until golden brown.
4. In a bowl, add all topping ingredients and mix well.
5. Spoon topping mixture over toasted bread slices and serve.

Nutritional Value (Amount per Serving):

- Calories 305
- Fat 19.6 g
- Carbohydrates 29.6 g
- Sugar 4.6 g
- Protein 6.4 g
- Cholesterol 0 mg

Mango Bruschetta

Preparation Time: 10 minutes
Cooking Time: 10 minutes
Serve: 8

Ingredients:

- 8 oz baguette bread, cut into 1-inch slices
- 2 tbsp olive oil

For topping:

- 1 tsp honey
- 2 tbsp olive oil
- 3 tbsp vinegar
- 2 garlic cloves, chopped
- 1/3 cup basil, chopped
- 1 mango, cubed
- 1 red bell pepper, chopped
- 4 yellow bell pepper, chopped

Directions:

1. Preheat Panini press.
2. Brush bread slices with oil and place on a hot Panini press. In batches.
3. Close Panini press and cook for 8-10 minutes or until golden brown.
4. In a bowl, add all topping ingredients and mix well.
5. Spoon topping mixture over toasted bread slices and serve.

Nutritional Value (Amount per Serving):

- Calories 189
- Fat 7.4 g
- Carbohydrates 27.4 g
- Sugar 10.8 g
- Protein 4.1 g
- Cholesterol 0 mg

Garlic Avocado Lime Bruschetta

Preparation Time: 10 minutes
Cooking Time: 10 minutes
Serve: 8

Ingredients:

- 8 oz baguette bread, cut into 1-inch slices
- 2 tbsp olive oil

For topping:

- 3 avocados, diced
- 1 tbsp garlic, minced
- 2 tbsp olive oil
- 3 tbsp fresh lime juice
- 3 tbsp scallions, minced
- 3 tbsp cilantro, chopped
- Pepper
- Salt

Directions:

1. Preheat Panini press.
2. Brush bread slices with oil and place on a hot Panini press. In batches.
3. Close Panini press and cook for 8-10 minutes or until golden brown.
4. In a bowl, add all topping ingredients and mix well.
5. Spoon topping mixture over toasted bread slices and serve.

Nutritional Value (Amount per Serving):

- Calories 291
- Fat 21.7 g
- Carbohydrates 21.5 g
- Sugar 1 g
- Protein 4.4 g
- Cholesterol 0 mg

Avocado Tomato Bruschetta

Preparation Time: 10 minutes
Cooking Time: 10 minutes
Serve: 6

Ingredients:

- 6 French bread slices
- 2 tbsp olive oil

For topping:

- 2 tomatoes, chopped
- 1/2 avocado, diced
- 2 tbsp basil, chopped
- 2 tbsp parsley, chopped
- 1 garlic clove, grated
- Pepper
- Salt

Directions:

1. Preheat Panini press.
2. Brush bread slices with oil and place on a hot Panini press. In batches.
3. Close Panini press and cook for 8-10 minutes or until golden brown.
4. In a bowl, add all topping ingredients and mix well.
5. Spoon topping mixture over toasted bread slices and serve.

Nutritional Value (Amount per Serving):

- Calories 175
- Fat 8.6 g
- Carbohydrates 21.4 g
- Sugar 2 g
- Protein 4.5 g
- Cholesterol 0 mg

Guacamole Bruschetta

Preparation Time: 10 minutes
Cooking Time: 10 minutes
Serve: 8

Ingredients:

- 8 oz baguette bread, cut into 1-inch slices
- 2 tbsp olive oil
- For topping:

- 2 avocados, diced
- 1 tbsp basil, chopped
- 1 tsp garlic, minced
- 1 tsp lemon juice
- Pepper
- Salt

Directions:

1. Preheat Panini press.
2. Brush bread slices with oil and place on a hot Panini press. In batches.
3. Close Panini press and cook for 8-10 minutes or until golden brown.
4. In a bowl, add all topping ingredients and mix well.
5. Spoon topping mixture over toasted bread slices and serve.

Nutritional Value (Amount per Serving):

- Calories 209
- Fat 13.3 g
- Carbohydrates 18.9 g
- Sugar 0.8 g
- Protein 3.9 g
- Cholesterol 0 mg

Tomato Mozzarella Bruschetta

Preparation Time: 10 minutes
Cooking Time: 10 minutes
Serve: 8

Ingredients:

- 8 oz baguette bread, cut into 1-inch slices
- 2 tbsp olive oil
- For topping:
- 8 oz mozzarella cheese, cut into cubes
- 2 tbsp basil, chopped
- 1/4 tsp garlic powder
- 1 tbsp olive oil
- 4 tomatoes, chopped
- Pepper
- Salt

Directions:

1. Preheat Panini press.
2. Brush bread slices with oil and place on a hot Panini press. In batches.
3. Close Panini press and cook for 8-10 minutes or until golden brown.
4. In a bowl, add all topping ingredients and mix well.
5. Spoon topping mixture over toasted bread slices and serve.

Nutritional Value (Amount per Serving):

- Calories 212
- Fat 10.4 g
- Carbohydrates 18 g
- Sugar 2.2 g

- Protein 11.5 g
- Cholesterol 15 mg

Chapter 8: Burgers & Pizza

Pepperoni Pizza Panini

Preparation Time: 10 minutes
Cooking Time: 10 minutes
Serve: 3

Ingredients:

- 6 bread slices
- 3/4 cup marinara sauce
- 21 pepperoni slices
- 1 1/2 cups mozzarella cheese, shredded
- 3 tbsp butter

Directions:

1. Preheat Panini press.
2. Spread butter on one side of each bread slice.
3. Take 3 bread slices and spread with marinara sauce and top with pepperoni slices and cheese.
4. Cover with remaining bread slices. Make sure buttered side up.
5. Place 2 sandwiches on a hot Panini press.
6. Close Panini press and cook for 5 minutes or until golden brown.
7. Serve and enjoy.

Nutritional Value (Amount per Serving):

- Calories 434
- Fat 33.4 g
- Carbohydrates 18.2 g
- Sugar 6.3 g
- Protein 15.3 g
- Cholesterol 80 mg

Easy Cheesy Pizza Panini

Preparation Time: 10 minutes
Cooking Time: 15 minutes
Serve: 6

Ingredients:

- 12 bread slices
- 3 tbsp butter
- 3 oz pepperoni slices
- 16 oz mozzarella cheese, sliced
- 6 oz pizza sauce

Directions:

1. Preheat Panini press.
2. Spread butter on one side of each bread slice.
3. Take 6 bread slices and spread with pizza sauce and top with pepperoni slices and cheese.
4. Cover with remaining bread slices. Make sure buttered side up.
5. Place 2 sandwiches on a hot Panini press.
6. Close Panini press and cook for 5 minutes or until golden brown.
7. Serve and enjoy.

Nutritional Value (Amount per Serving):

- Calories 395
- Fat 25.5 g
- Carbohydrates 15.1 g
- Sugar 1.7 g
- Protein 26.1 g
- Cholesterol 69 mg

Classic Pizza Panini

Preparation Time: 10 minutes
Cooking Time: 5 minutes
Serve: 2

Ingredients:

- 4 bread slices
- 1 tbsp butter
- 4 tbsp pizza sauce
- 12 pepperoni slices
- 4 mozzarella cheese slices
- 2 tbsp olives, sliced

Directions:

1. Preheat Panini press.
2. Spread butter on one side of each bread slice.
3. Take 2 bread slices and spread with pizza sauce and top with pepperoni slices, olives, and cheese.
4. Cover with remaining bread slices. Make sure buttered side up.
5. Place sandwiches on a hot Panini press.
6. Close Panini press and cook for 5 minutes or until golden brown.
7. Serve and enjoy.

Nutritional Value (Amount per Serving):

- Calories 449
- Fat 32 g
- Carbohydrates 15.1 g
- Sugar 1.8 g
- Protein 25.5 g
- Cholesterol 80 mg

Pesto Pizza Panini

Preparation Time: 10 minutes
Cooking Time: 5 minutes
Serve: 2

Ingredients:

- 4 bread slices
- 1 tbsp butter
- 4 tbsp basil pesto
- 12 pepperoni slices
- 4 mozzarella cheese slices
- 2 tbsp olives, sliced

Directions:

1. Preheat Panini press.
2. Spread butter on one side of each bread slice.
3. Take 2 bread slices and spread with pesto and top with pepperoni slices, olives, and cheese.
4. Cover with remaining bread slices. Make sure buttered side up.
5. Place sandwiches on a hot Panini press.
6. Close Panini press and cook for 5 minutes or until golden brown.
7. Serve and enjoy.

Nutritional Value (Amount per Serving):

- Calories 433
- Fat 31.8 g
- Carbohydrates 11.8 g
- Sugar 0.8 g
- Protein 25.2 g
- Cholesterol 80 mg

Chicken Pizza Panini

Preparation Time: 10 minutes
Cooking Time: 5 minutes
Serve: 2

Ingredients:

- 4 bread slices
- 1 tbsp butter
- 1 chicken breast, cooked and sliced
- 2 tbsp marinara sauce
- 12 pepperoni slices
- 4 mozzarella cheese slices
- 2 tbsp olives, sliced

Directions:

1. Preheat Panini press.
2. Spread butter on one side of each bread slice.
3. Take 2 bread slices and spread with marinara sauce and top with chicken, pepperoni slices, olives, and cheese.
4. Cover with remaining bread slices. Make sure buttered side up.
5. Place sandwiches on a hot Panini press.
6. Close Panini press and cook for 5 minutes or until golden brown.
7. Serve and enjoy.

Nutritional Value (Amount per Serving):

- Calories 502
- Fat 33.4 g
- Carbohydrates 13.8 g
- Sugar 2.2 g
- Protein 35.9 g
- Cholesterol 112 mg

Cottage Cheese Pizza Panini

Preparation Time: 10 minutes
Cooking Time: 5 minutes
Serve: 2

Ingredients:

- 4 bread slices
- 1 tbsp butter
- 2 tbsp pizza sauce
- 12 pepperoni slices
- 4 tbsp cottage cheese, crumbled
- 4 mozzarella cheese slices
- 2 tbsp olives, sliced

Directions:

1. Preheat Panini press.
2. Spread butter on one side of each bread slice.
3. Take 2 bread slices and spread with pizza sauce and top with cottage cheese, pepperoni slices, olives, and cheese.
4. Cover with remaining bread slices. Make sure buttered side up.
5. Place sandwiches on a hot Panini press.
6. Close Panini press and cook for 5 minutes or until golden brown.
7. Serve and enjoy.

Nutritional Value (Amount per Serving):

- Calories 466
- Fat 32.4 g
- Carbohydrates 14.4 g
- Sugar 1.4 g
- Protein 29.1 g
- Cholesterol 82 mg

Chicken Burger Patties

Preparation Time: 10 minutes
Cooking Time: 12 minutes
Serve: 6

Ingredients:

- 1 lb ground chicken
- 1 tsp ground cumin
- 1/2 tsp cayenne
- 1 1/2 tbsp chili powder
- 1/2 red pepper, diced
- 1 small onion, diced
- 1/2 cup basked tortilla chips, crushed
- Salt

Directions:

1. Preheat Panini press.
2. Add all ingredients into the mixing bowl and mix until well combined.
3. Make 6 patties from the mixture and spray with cooking spray.
4. Place patties on hot Panini press and cook for 4-6 minutes on each side.
5. Serve and enjoy.

Nutritional Value (Amount per Serving):

- Calories 171
- Fat 6.6 g
- Carbohydrates 4.7 g
- Sugar 1.2 g
- Protein 22.6 g
- Cholesterol 67 mg

Chili Honey Chicken Burger Patties

Preparation Time: 10 minutes
Cooking Time: 12 minutes
Serve: 6

Ingredients:

- 1 lb ground chicken
- 1/4 cup almond meal
- 1/4 tsp pepper
- 2 tsp dried parsley
- 1 tsp paprika
- 1 tsp chili powder
- 1 tsp cayenne powder
- 1 tbsp honey
- 1/4 tsp salt

Directions:

1. Preheat Panini press.

2. Add all ingredients into the mixing bowl and mix until well combined.
3. Make 6 patties from the mixture and spray with cooking spray.
4. Place patties on hot Panini press and cook for 4-6 minutes on each side.
5. Serve and enjoy.

Nutritional Value (Amount per Serving):

- Calories 181
- Fat 7.8 g
- Carbohydrates 4.4 g
- Sugar 3.1 g
- Protein 22.9 g
- Cholesterol 67 mg

Cilantro Lime Chicken Burger Patties

Preparation Time: 10 minutes
Cooking Time: 12 minutes
Serve: 6

Ingredients:

- 1 lb ground chicken
- 1/4 tsp pepper
- 1/2 tbsp ground cumin
- 3 garlic cloves, minced
- 1/3 cup cilantro, chopped
- 1 lime juice
- 1/2 tsp salt

Directions:

1. Preheat Panini press.
2. Add all ingredients into the mixing bowl and mix until well combined.
3. Make 6 patties from the mixture and spray with cooking spray.
4. Place patties on hot Panini press and cook for 4-6 minutes on each side.
5. Serve and enjoy.

Nutritional Value (Amount per Serving):

- Calories 150
- Fat 5.7 g
- Carbohydrates 1.4 g
- Sugar 0.2 g
- Protein 22.1 g
- Cholesterol 67 mg

Easy Beef Burger Patties

Preparation Time: 10 minutes
Cooking Time: 10 minutes
Serve: 4

Ingredients:

- 1 lb ground beef
- 3/4 tbsp Worcestershire sauce
- 1 tbsp Dijon mustard
- 1/2 tsp pepper
- 1/2 tsp kosher salt

Directions:

1. Preheat Panini press.
2. Add all ingredients into the mixing bowl and mix until well combined.
3. Make 4 patties from the mixture and spray with cooking spray.
4. Place patties on hot Panini press and cook for 4-5 minutes on each side.
5. Serve and enjoy.

Nutritional Value (Amount per Serving):

- Calories 217
- Fat 7.2 g
- Carbohydrates 0.9 g
- Sugar 0.6 g
- Protein 34.6 g
- Cholesterol 101 mg

Chapter 9: Miscellaneous

Grilled Pineapple Slices

Preparation Time: 10 minutes
Cooking Time: 12 minutes
Serve: 4

Ingredients:

- 4 pineapple slices
- 1 tbsp olive oil
- Salt

Directions:

1. Preheat Panini press.
2. Brush pineapple slices with oil and season with salt.
3. Place pineapple slices on hot Panini press and cook for 5-6 minutes on each side.
4. Serve and enjoy.

Nutritional Value (Amount per Serving):

- Calories 112
- Fat 3.7 g
- Carbohydrates 21.7 g
- Sugar 16.3 g
- Protein 0.9 g
- Cholesterol 0 mg

Spicy Chicken Thighs

Preparation Time: 10 minutes
Cooking Time: 12 minutes
Serve: 4

Ingredients:

- 4 chicken thighs, skinless
- 1 tsp fish sauce
- 1 tsp soy sauce
- 1/3 cup sweet chili sauce
- 2 tsp lemongrass, minced
- 1/2 tsp ginger, minced
- Pepper
- Salt

Directions:

1. Add all ingredients except chicken into the zip-lock bag and mix well.
2. Add chicken into the bag, seal bag shakes well, and place in the fridge overnight.
3. Preheat Panini press.
4. Place chicken thigh on hot Panini press and cook for 6 minutes on each side.

5. Serve and enjoy.

Nutritional Value (Amount per Serving):

- Calories 320
- Fat 10.8 g
- Carbohydrates 8.5 g
- Sugar 8.1 g
- Protein 42.4 g
- Cholesterol 130 mg

Juicy Chicken Breast

Preparation Time: 10 minutes
Cooking Time: 12 minutes
Serve: 4

Ingredients:

- 4 chicken breasts
- 1/2 tsp ground coriander
- 1 tsp ground cumin
- 1 tsp garlic powder
- 2 tbsp olive oil
- 1/2 tsp smoked paprika
- 1/4 tsp pepper
- 1/2 tsp sea salt

Directions:

1. Preheat Panini press.
2. In a small bowl, mix oil, paprika, coriander, cumin, garlic powder, pepper, and salt and rub all over the chicken breasts.
3. Place chicken on hot Panini press and cook for 6 minutes on each side.
4. Serve and enjoy.

Nutritional Value (Amount per Serving):

- Calories 345
- Fat 18 g
- Carbohydrates 1 g
- Sugar 0.2 g
- Protein 42.5 g
- Cholesterol 130 mg

Easy Lemon Pepper Chicken

Preparation Time: 10 minutes
Cooking Time: 20 minutes
Serve: 6

Ingredients:

- 6 chicken breast, boneless
- 2 tsp garlic, minced
- 1/2 cup olive oil
- 2 lemon juice

- 1/2 onion, diced
- 1 tsp pepper
- 1 tsp salt

Directions:

1. Add all ingredients except chicken into the zip-lock bag and mix well.
2. Add chicken into the bag, seal bag shakes well, and place in the refrigerator overnight.
3. Preheat Panini press.
4. Place chicken on hot Panini press and cook for 20 minutes on each side. Flip chicken breast after every 5 minutes.
5. Serve and enjoy.

Nutritional Value (Amount per Serving):

- Calories 430
- Fat 27.8 g
- Carbohydrates 1.7 g
- Sugar 0.7 g
- Protein 42.6 g
- Cholesterol 130 mg

Cauliflower Steaks

Preparation Time: 10 minutes
Cooking Time: 10 minutes
Serve: 4

Ingredients:

- 1 medium cauliflower head, cut into 1/2-inch thick slices
- 1/2 tsp lemon pepper seasoning
- 1/2 tsp dried thyme
- 2 tbsp soy sauce
- 4 garlic cloves, minced
- 1/2 cup parmesan cheese, grated
- 1/2 tsp onion powder
- 1/2 tsp chili powder
- 1/4 cup olive oil
- Pepper
- Salt

Directions:

1. In a small bowl, mix onion powder, chili powder, lemon pepper seasoning, thyme, soy sauce, garlic, olive oil, pepper, and salt.
2. Brush cauliflower slices with spice and oil mixture.
3. Preheat Panini press.
4. Place cauliflower slices on hot Panini press and cook for 5 minutes on each side.
5. Sprinkle with cheese and serve.

Nutritional Value (Amount per Serving):

- Calories 155
- Fat 12.9 g
- Carbohydrates 10 g
- Sugar 3.8 g
- Protein 3.7 g
- Cholesterol 0 mg

Grill Sweet Potatoes

Preparation Time: 10 minutes
Cooking Time: 6 minutes
Serve: 4

Ingredients:

- 2 large sweet potatoes, sliced thinly
- 1tsp garlic powder
- 1 tsp chili powder
- 1 1/2 tbsp olive oil
- 1/4 tsp chipotle chili powder
- 1/2 tsp cumin
- 1/2 tsp paprika

Directions:

1. Preheat Panini press.
2. Add sweet potato slices and remaining ingredients into the mixing bowl and toss well.
3. Place sweet potato slices in batches on hot Panini press and cook for 3 minutes on each side.
4. Serve and enjoy.

Nutritional Value (Amount per Serving):

- Calories 80
- Fat 5.5 g
- Carbohydrates 7.7 g
- Sugar 1.6 g
- Protein 0.8 g
- Cholesterol 0 mg

Marinated Broccoli

Preparation Time: 10 minutes
Cooking Time: 6 minutes
Serve: 6

Ingredients:

- 4 cups broccoli florets
- 1 tbsp lemon juice
- 4 tbsp olive oil
- 1/4 tsp pepper
- 1 1/2 tsp garlic, minced
- 1 1/2 tsp Italian seasoning
- 1 1/4 tsp kosher salt

Directions:

1. Add broccoli and remaining ingredients into the mixing bowl and mix well. Cover and place in the refrigerator for 2 hours.
2. Preheat Panini press.
3. Place broccoli florets in batches on hot Panini press and cook for 3 minutes on each side.
4. Serve and enjoy.

Nutritional Value (Amount per Serving):

- Calories 105
- Fat 9.9 g
- Carbohydrates 4.5 g
- Sugar 1.2 g
- Protein 1.8 g
- Cholesterol 1 mg

Grill Salmon Patties

Preparation Time: 10 minutes
Cooking Time: 8 minutes
Serve: 6

Ingredients:

- 2 eggs
- 1 lb salmon fillet, remove skin
- 1/4 cup fresh parsley, chopped
- 1 cup breadcrumbs
- 1 tsp mustard
- 1 tbsp fresh lemon juice
- 1/4 cup mayonnaise
- 1/2 tsp pepper
- 1/2 tsp salt

Directions:

1. Preheat Panini press.
2. Add all ingredients into the bowl and mix until well combined.
3. Make 6 patties from the mixture.
4. Place patties on hot Panini press and cook for 4 minutes on each side.
5. Serve and enjoy.

Nutritional Value (Amount per Serving):

- Calories 236
- Fat 10.6 g
- Carbohydrates 15.9 g
- Sugar 2 g
- Protein 19.3 g
- Cholesterol 90 mg

Lemon Pepper Salmon

Preparation Time: 10 minutes
Cooking Time: 8 minutes
Serve: 4

Ingredients:

- 1 1/2 lbs salmon fillets
- 1/4 cup olive oil
- 1 lemon juice
- 1 tsp dried oregano
- 2 garlic cloves, minced
- 1/2 tsp pepper
- 1 tsp sea salt

Directions:

1. In a large bowl, mix oregano, garlic, oil, lemon juice, pepper, and salt. Add salmon fillets and coat well. Cover and place in the refrigerator for 15 minutes.
2. Preheat Panini press.
3. Place marinated salmon fillets on hot Panini press and cook for 4 minutes on each side.
4. Serve and enjoy.

Nutritional Value (Amount per Serving):

- Calories 335
- Fat 23.2 g
- Carbohydrates 0.9 g
- Sugar 0 g
- Protein 33.2 g
- Cholesterol 75 mg

Grill Mahi Mahi Fish Fillets

Preparation Time: 10 minutes
Cooking Time: 10 minutes
Serve: 3

Ingredients:

- 3 mahi-mahi fillets
- 1/8 tsp cayenne pepper
- 1/2 tsp onion powder
- 1/2 tsp garlic powder
- 2 tbsp fresh lemon juice
- 1 tsp cumin
- 1 tsp dried oregano
- 1 tsp paprika
- 3 tbsp olive oil
- 1/4 tsp pepper
- 1/2 tsp salt

Directions:

1. Preheat Panini press.
2. In a small bowl, mix cumin, oregano, cayenne, garlic powder, paprika, pepper, and salt.
3. Brush fish fillets with oil and season with spice mixture.
4. Place fish fillets on hot Panini press and cook for 5 minutes on each side.
5. Drizzle fish fillets with lemon juice and serve.

Nutritional Value (Amount per Serving):

- Calories 165
- Fat 14.4 g
- Carbohydrates 2.1 g
- Sugar 0.6 g
- Protein 7.5 g
- Cholesterol 13 mg

Grill Cod

Preparation Time: 10 minutes
Cooking Time: 8 minutes
Serve: 4

Ingredients:

- 4 cod fillets
- 1 tbsp olive oil
- 2 tbsp blackened seasoning
- 1/2 tsp kosher salt

Directions:

1. Preheat Panini press.
2. Brush cod fillets with oil and season with blackened seasoning and kosher salt.
3. Place fish fillets on hot Panini press and cook for 4 minutes on each side.
4. Serve and enjoy.

Nutritional Value (Amount per Serving):

- Calories 151
- Fat 4 g
- Carbohydrates 19 g
- Sugar 0 g
- Protein 10 g
- Cholesterol 15 mg

Easy Lamb Patties

Preparation Time: 10 minutes
Cooking Time: 12 minutes
Serve: 4

Ingredients:

- 1 lb ground lamb
- 1 tsp ground cumin
- 1/4 tsp cayenne pepper
- 1/4 cup fresh parsley, chopped
- 1/4 cup onion, minced
- 1/4 tsp pepper
- 1 tsp ground cinnamon
- 1 tbsp garlic, chopped
- 1/2 tsp ground allspice
- 1 tsp ground coriander
- 1 tsp kosher salt

Directions:

1. Preheat Panini press.
2. Add all ingredients into the mixing bowl and mix until well combined.
3. Make 4 patties from the mixture and spray with cooking spray.
4. Place patties on hot Panini press and cook for 6 minutes on each side.
5. Serve and enjoy.

Nutritional Value (Amount per Serving):

- Calories 226
- Fat 8 g
- Carbohydrates 2.6 g
- Sugar 0.4 g
- Protein 32 g
- Cholesterol 102 mg

Grill Lamb Chops

Preparation Time: 10 minutes
Cooking Time: 10 minutes
Serve: 4

Ingredients:

- 8 lamb loin chops
- 6 garlic cloves, crushed
- 1 tsp olive oil
- 1/4 tsp black pepper
- 1 tbsp fresh rosemary, chopped
- 1/4 cup fresh lemon juice
- 1 1/4 tsp kosher salt

Directions:

1. Add all ingredients except pork chops into the zip-lock bag and mix well.
2. Add pork chops into the bag, seal bag shakes well, and place in the refrigerator overnight.
3. Preheat Panini press.
4. Place marinated lamb chops on hot Panini press and cook for 5 minutes on each side.
5. Serve and enjoy.

Nutritional Value (Amount per Serving):

- Calories 390
- Fat 17.4 g
- Carbohydrates 2.4 g
- Sugar 0.4 g
- Protein 50.5 g
- Cholesterol 160 mg

Grill Pork Chops

Preparation Time: 10 minutes
Cooking Time: 14 minutes
Serve: 2

Ingredients:

- 2 pork chops
- For marinade:
- 1/3 cup olive oil
- 1/2 tsp oregano
- 1 tsp onion powder
- 1 tbsp brown sugar
- 1/4 cup soy sauce
- 1/4 cup fresh lemon juice
- Pepper
- Salt

Directions:

1. Add all marinade ingredients into the zip-lock bag and mix well.
2. Add pork chops into the zip-lock bag, seal bag shake well and place in the refrigerator for overnight.
3. Preheat Panini press.
4. Place pork chops on hot Panini press and cook for 7 minutes on each side.
5. Serve and enjoy.

Nutritional Value (Amount per Serving):

- Calories 590
- Fat 53.8 g
- Carbohydrates 8.7 g
- Sugar 6 g
- Protein 20.4 g
- Cholesterol 69 mg

Savory Pork Chops

Preparation Time: 10 minutes
Cooking Time: 12 minutes
Serve:

Ingredients:

- 4 pork loin chops
- For rub:

- 2 tbsp brown sugar
- 1 tsp black pepper
- 1/2 tsp cayenne pepper
- 1/2 tsp ground mustard
- 1 tsp paprika
- 2 tsp kosher salt

Directions:

1. Preheat Panini press.
2. In a small bowl mix rub ingredients and rub all over pork chops.
3. Place pork chops on hot Panini press and cook for 6 minutes on each side.
4. Serve and enjoy.

Nutritional Value (Amount per Serving):

- Calories 280
- Fat 20.1 g
- Carbohydrates 5.3 g
- Sugar 4.5 g
- Protein 18.3 g
- Cholesterol 69 mg

Easy Beef Burger Patties

Preparation Time: 10 minutes
Cooking Time: 12 minutes
Serve: 4

Ingredients:

- 1 lb ground beef
- 1 tsp garlic, minced
- 1 tbsp steak sauce
- Pepper
- Salt

Directions:

1. Preheat Panini press.
2. Add all ingredients into the mixing bowl and mix until well combined.
3. Make 4 patties from the mixture and spray with cooking spray.
4. Place patties on hot Panini press and cook for 6 minutes on each side.
5. Serve and enjoy.

Nutritional Value (Amount per Serving):

- Calories 210
- Fat 7.1 g
- Carbohydrates 0.3 g
- Sugar 0 g
- Protein 34.4 g
- Cholesterol 101 mg

Grill Short Ribs

Preparation Time: 10 minutes
Cooking Time: 10 minutes
Serve: 4

Ingredients:

- 1 lb flanken cut short ribs
- For marinade:
- 1/2 medium onion
- 1 tbsp sesame oil
- 1/2 cup sugar
- 1/2 cup soy sauce
- 1/2 tbsp pepper
- The 1/4-inch ginger piece, peeled
- 5 garlic cloves
- 1/2 pear, peeled & cored

Directions:

1. Add all marinade ingredients into the blender and blend until well combined.
2. Add ribs into the zip-lock bag then pour marinade over ribs, seal bag shake well, and place in the fridge for overnight.
3. Preheat Panini press.
4. Place short ribs on hot Panini press and cook for 5 minutes on each side.
5. Serve and enjoy.

Nutritional Value (Amount per Serving):

- Calories 476
- Fat 29.6 g
- Carbohydrates 33.1 g
- Sugar 27.9 g
- Protein 21.6 g
- Cholesterol 75 mg

Marinated Steak

Preparation Time: 10 minutes
Cooking Time: 12 minutes
Serve: 4

Ingredients:

- 4 ribeye steaks
- 1 1/2 tbsp garlic powder
- 1/4 cup Worcestershire sauce
- 1 lemon juice
- 1 tsp ground white pepper
- 3 tbsp dried basil
- 1/2 cup olive oil
- 1/3 cup soy sauce

Directions:

1. Add all ingredients except steaks into the zip-lock bag and mix well.
2. Add steaks into the bag, seal bag shakes well, and place in the fridge overnight.
3. Preheat Panini press.
4. Place steaks on hot Panini press and cook for 6 minutes on each side.
5. Serve and enjoy.

Nutritional Value (Amount per Serving):

- Calories 890
- Fat 69.4 g
- Carbohydrates 7.6 g
- Sugar 4.4 g
- Protein 2.1 g
- Cholesterol 0 mg

Greek Chicken

Preparation Time: 10 minutes
Cooking Time: 12 minutes
Serve: 4

Ingredients:

- 4 chicken breasts
- 6 tbsp fresh parsley, minced
- 6 tbsp olive oil
- 6 tbsp fresh lemon juice
- 1 1/2 tsp dried oregano
- 1 tsp paprika
- 6 garlic cloves, minced
- Pepper
- Salt

Directions:

1. Add all ingredients except chicken into the zip-lock bag and mix well.
2. Add chicken into the bag, seal bag shakes well, and place in the fridge overnight.
3. Preheat Panini press.
4. Place chicken on hot Panini press and cook for 6 minutes on each side.
5. Serve and enjoy.

Nutritional Value (Amount per Serving):

- Calories 475
- Fat 32.2 g
- Carbohydrates 3 g
- Sugar 0.7 g
- Protein 43 g
- Cholesterol 130 mg

Turkey Spinach Burgers

Preparation Time: 10 minutes
Cooking Time: 10 minutes

Serve: 4

Ingredients:

- 1 lb ground turkey
- 1/2 cup feta cheese, crumbled
- 1 tbsp almond flour
- 1/4 tsp crushed red pepper
- 1 tsp parsley
- 1 tsp oregano
- 1 tsp garlic powder
- 1/3 cup sun-dried tomatoes
- 1/2 cup baby spinach, chopped
- 1/2 tsp pepper
- 1/2 tsp sea salt

Directions:

1. Preheat Panini press.
2. Add all ingredients into the mixing bowl and mix until well combined.
3. Make 4 patties from the mixture and spray with cooking spray.
4. Place patties on hot Panini press and cook for 5 minutes on each side.
5. Serve and enjoy.

Nutritional Value (Amount per Serving):

- Calories 290
- Fat 17.4 g
- Carbohydrates 2.9 g
- Sugar 1.4 g
- Protein 34.5 g
- Cholesterol 132 mg

Grill Chicken Drumsticks

Preparation Time: 10 minutes
Cooking Time: 30 minutes
Serve: 8

Ingredients:

- 2 lbs chicken legs
- 2 tbsp olive oil
- 2 tbsp taco seasoning

Directions:

1. Preheat Panini press.
2. Brush chicken legs with oil and rub with taco seasoning.
3. Place chicken legs in batches on hot Panini press and cook for 30 minutes on each side. Turn chicken legs after every 10 minutes.
4. Serve and enjoy.

Nutritional Value (Amount per Serving):

- Calories 246
- Fat 11.9 g
- Carbohydrates 0 g
- Sugar 0 g
- Protein 32.8 g
- Cholesterol 101 mg

Bacon Turkey Burgers

Preparation Time: 10 minutes
Cooking Time: 8 minutes
Serve: 5

Ingredients:

- 1 lb ground turkey
- 1/2 tsp garlic powder
- 1/3 cup bacon, chopped
- 1/3 cup green onions, chopped
- 1 cup cheddar cheese, shredded
- 1/4 cup BBQ sauce
- Pepper
- Salt

Directions:

1. Preheat Panini press.
2. Add all ingredients into the mixing bowl and mix until well combined.
3. Make 5 patties from the mixture and spray with cooking spray.
4. Place patties on hot Panini press and cook for 4 minutes on each side.
5. Serve and enjoy.

Nutritional Value (Amount per Serving):

- Calories 290
- Fat 17 g
- Carbohydrates 5 g
- Sugar 3.6 g
- Protein 30.6 g
- Cholesterol 116 mg

Spicy Chicken

Preparation Time: 10 minutes
Cooking Time: 12 minutes
Serve: 4

Ingredients:

- 4 chicken breasts
- 2 tbsp olive oil
- 1/2 tsp smoked paprika
- 1 tsp ground cumin
- 1 tsp garlic powder
- 1/4 tsp black pepper
- 1/2 tsp ground coriander
- 1/2 tsp sea salt

Directions:

1. Preheat Panini press.
2. In a small bowl, mix together garlic powder, oil, pepper, paprika, coriander, cumin, and salt and rub all over the chicken.
3. Place chicken on hot Panini press and cook for 6 minutes on each side.
4. Serve and enjoy.

Nutritional Value (Amount per Serving):

- Calories 345
- Fat 18 g
- Carbohydrates 1 g
- Sugar 0.2 g
- Protein 42.5 g
- Cholesterol 130 mg

Easy Grill Chicken Breast

Preparation Time: 10 minutes
Cooking Time: 10 minutes
Serve: 2

Ingredients:

- 2 chicken breasts, boneless
- 1 tsp garlic powder
- 2 tbsp soy sauce
- 2 tbsp olive oil
- 1/4 tsp black pepper

Directions:

1. Add chicken into the zip-lock bag.
2. In a small bowl, mix together olive oil, soy sauce, garlic powder, and pepper and pour over the chicken.
3. Seal bag and place in the refrigerator overnight.
4. Preheat Panini press.
5. Place chicken on hot Panini press and cook for 5 minutes on each side.
6. Serve and enjoy.

Nutritional Value (Amount per Serving):

- Calories 410
- Fat 24 g
- Carbohydrates 2.4 g
- Sugar 0.6 g
- Protein 43.5 g
- Cholesterol 130 mg

Grill Zucchini

Preparation Time: 10 minutes
Cooking Time: 10 minutes

Serve: 4

Ingredients:

- 16 oz zucchini, sliced 1/4-inch thick
- 1 tbsp olive oil
- 1/2 tsp garlic powder
- 1 tsp dried basil
- 1 tsp dried parsley
- 1 tbsp red wine vinegar
- Pepper
- Salt

Directions:

1. Preheat Panini press.
2. Add zucchini slices and remaining ingredients into the mixing bowl and toss well.
3. Place zucchini slices in batches on hot Panini press and cook for 2-3 minutes on each side.
4. Serve and enjoy.

Nutritional Value (Amount per Serving):

- Calories 50
- Fat 3.7 g
- Carbohydrates 4.1 g
- Sugar 2.1 g
- Protein 1.5 g
- Cholesterol 0 mg

Cauliflower Wedges

Preparation Time: 10 minutes
Cooking Time: 20 minutes
Serve: 8

Ingredients:

- 1 large cauliflower head, cut into 8 wedges
- 1/2 tsp crushed red pepper flakes
- 1/2 tsp ground turmeric
- 2 tbsp olive oil

Directions:

1. Preheat Panini press.
2. Brush cauliflower wedges with oil and sprinkle with turmeric and crushed red pepper flakes.
3. Place cauliflower wedges on hot Panini press and cook for 10 minutes on each side.
4. Serve and enjoy.

Nutritional Value (Amount per Serving):

- Calories 55
- Fat 3.6 g

- Carbohydrates 5.7 g
- Sugar 2.5 g
- Protein 2.1 g
- Cholesterol 0 mg

Grill Lamb Chops

Preparation Time: 10 minutes
Cooking Time: 8 minutes
Serve: 6

Ingredients:

- 6 lamb chops
- 2 tbsp fresh mint, chopped
- 1/2 tsp Pepper
- 2 tbsp olive oil
- 1/2 tsp kosher salt

Directions:

1. Preheat Panini press.
2. Brush lamb chops with oil and season with pepper and salt.
3. Place lamb chops on hot Panini press and cook for 4 minutes on each side.
4. Garnish with mint.
5. Serve and enjoy.

Nutritional Value (Amount per Serving):

- Calories 300
- Fat 19.7 g
- Carbohydrates 5 g
- Sugar 0 g
- Protein 25 g
- Cholesterol 0 mg

Herb Beef Burger Patties

Preparation Time: 10 minutes
Cooking Time: 8 minutes
Serve: 5

Ingredients:

- 1 lb ground beef
- 1 egg, lightly beaten
- 2 tbsp fresh parsley, chopped
- 1 tsp dry oregano
- 1 tsp dry mint
- 3 tbsp almond flour
- 1 small onion, grated
- Pepper
- Salt

Directions:

1. Preheat Panini press.
2. Add all ingredients into the mixing bowl and mix until well combined.
3. Make 5 patties from the mixture and spray with cooking spray.
4. Place patties on hot Panini press and cook for 4 minutes on each side.
5. Serve and enjoy.

Nutritional Value (Amount per Serving):

- Calories 285
- Fat 15 g
- Carbohydrates 5.3 g
- Sugar 1.3 g
- Protein 32.5 g
- Cholesterol 114 mg

Grill Burger Patties

Preparation Time: 10 minutes
Cooking Time: 10 minutes
Serve: 6

Ingredients:

- 1 lb ground lamb
- 1 tsp cumin
- 1/2 cup green onion, chopped
- 2 tbsp olive oil
- 1 tsp dried rosemary
- 1 lb ground beef
- 1 tbsp dried oregano
- 1 tbsp dried thyme
- 1 tsp pepper
- 1 1/2 tsp salt

Directions:

1. Preheat Panini press.
2. Add all ingredients into the mixing bowl and mix until well combined.
3. Make 6 patties from the mixture and spray with cooking spray.
4. Place patties on hot Panini press and cook for 5 minutes on each side.
5. Serve and enjoy.

Nutritional Value (Amount per Serving):

- Calories 331
- Fat 15.2 g
- Carbohydrates 1.9 g
- Sugar 0.2 g
- Protein 44.5 g
- Cholesterol 136 mg

Salmon Patties

Preparation Time: 10 minutes
Cooking Time: 10 minutes

Serve: 2

Ingredients:

- 8 oz salmon fillet, minced
- 1 egg, lightly beaten
- 2 tbsp breadcrumbs
- 1/4 tsp garlic powder
- Pepper
- Salt

Directions:

1. Preheat Panini press.
2. Add all ingredients into the bowl and mix until just combined.
3. Make small patties from the salmon mixture. Spray patties from the cooking spray.
4. Place salmon patties on hot Panini press and cook for 4-5 minutes on each side.
5. Serve and enjoy.

Nutritional Value (Amount per Serving):

- Calories 185
- Fat 9.2 g
- Carbohydrates 0.5 g
- Sugar 0.3 g
- Protein 24.8 g
- Cholesterol 132 mg

Conclusion

The Hamilton Panini Press Grill is one of the simple and versatile cooking appliances available in the market. It looks simple but attractive and having non-stick cooking surfaces on the top and bottom cooking surface area. It comes with a compact size and doesn't take much space over your kitchen top. It is capable to hold 2 to 3 sandwiches at a time over its 10 inches by 8-inch cooking surface area. It is one of the safest cooking appliances comes with a large cool-touch pressing handle on its top lid portion. The outer portion of the appliances comes with a nice chrome finish. It cooks your sandwiches faster and also saves your cooking time and efforts.

This cookbook contains tasty, healthy and delicious Panini recipes selected from the different categories like breakfast Panini's, vegetable Panini's, poultry Panini's, Beef & lamb Panini's, pork Panini's, bruschetta, burgers & pizza and miscellaneous. All these recipes are unique and written into an easily understandable form. All the recipes come with preparation and cooking time information. The book also contains step by step information with cooking instructions. Finally, all the recipes end with their nutritional value information.